คopyrighted material

Vietnam Travel Guide 2025

Exploring the Hidden Hill Tribes, Colonial Heritage, and Culinary Delights of Vietnam's Diverse Regions

Richard B. Rose

copyrighted material

copyright © 2025, Richard B. Rose

All rights reserved. No part of this travel guide may be reproduced, distributed, or transmitted in any form or by any means, including photocopying, recording, or other electronic or mechanical methods, without the prior written permission of the publisher, except in the case of brief quotations embodied in critical reviews and cert... write to the publisher

Disclaimer

While every effort has been made to ensure the accuracy of the information contained in this guide, the author and publisher assume no responsibility for errors, omissions, or changes in details. The information provided is for general informational purposes only and should not be considered as professional advice. Travelers are encouraged to verify all details with the relevant authorities and service providers before making any travel arrangements.

Table of Contents

Introduction — 7
- **Welcome to Vietnam** — 7
  - Overview of Vietnam — 7
- **Why Visit Vietnam in 2025** — 7
- **Quick Facts about Vietnam** — 8
  - Geography, Population, and Culture — 8

Chapter 1: Planning Your Trip — 11
- **When to Visit Vietnam** — 11
  - Best Seasons to Travel — 11
- **Festivals and Events** — 13
- **Visa and Entry Requirements** — 18
- **Getting There** — 24
- **Entry Points and Border Crossings** — 30
- **Travel Insurance** — 31

Chapter 2: Exploring Vietnam — 35
- **Top Destinations** — 35
- **Itineraries** — 38
  - 7-Day Itinerary — 38
  - 10-Day Itinerary — 39
  - 14-Day Itinerary — 43
  - Beach Holidays Itinerary — 52

Chapter 3: Accommodations — 56
- **Hotels and Resorts** — 56
  - Luxury Hotels and Resorts — 56
  - Mid-Range Hotels — 59
  - Boutique Hotels — 61
  - Budget Hotels — 63
- **Guesthouses and Hostels** — 65
  - Guesthouses — 65
  - Hostels — 67
- **Homestays** — 69
- **Accommodation Tips** — 71
- **Budgeting for Accommodation:** — 72
- **Getting Around Vietnam** — 73
  - Domestic Flights — 73

Trains and Rail Travel	75
Buses and Coaches	76
Taxis and Ride-Sharing Services	77

Chapter 4: Transportation — 79

Travel Tips	79
Navigating Public Transportation	79
Renting Vehicles	80
Vietnamese Cuisine	81
Must-Try Dishes	81
Street Food Delights	82
Dining Etiquette	84
Drinks and Nightlife	85
Popular Beverages	85
Best Bars and Nightclubs	86
Local Etiquette	88

Chapter 6: Activities and Adventures — 90

Outdoor Adventures	90
Hiking and Trekking	90
Water Sports	91
Cycling Tours	92

Chapter 7: Activities and Adventures — 94

Cultural Experiences	94
Visiting Temples and Pagodas	94
Traditional Performances	95
Festivals and Celebrations	97

Chapter 8: Shopping in Vietnam — 99

Best Shopping Destinations	99
Markets and Bazaars	99
Shopping Malls and Boutiques	100
Artisan Shops	102
Souvenirs and Handicrafts	103
Local Products	104
Shopping Tips and Bargaining	105

Chapter 9: Culture and Etiquette — 107

Understanding Vietnamese Culture	107
Key Cultural Norms and Social Etiquette	107
Language Tips	108

Common Phrases and Greetings	109
Basic Vietnamese for Travelers	110
Chapter 10: Health and Safety	**111**
Staying Healthy	113
Recommended Vaccinations	113
Medical Facilities and Pharmacies	114
Health and Safety Tips	115
Staying Safe	116
General Safety Tips	116
Common Scams and How to Avoid Them	118
Emergency Contacts and Services	119
Chapter 11: Practical Information	**120**
Money Matters	120
Currency and Exchange	122
Banking and ATMs	123
Tipping Etiquette	123
Communication and Connectivity	124
Mobile Networks and Internet Access	124
Useful Apps for Travelers	125
Staying Connected	126
Sustainable Travel Tips	127
Eco-Friendly Practices	128
Supporting Local Communities	129
Appendix	**130**
Useful Apps	130
Conclusion	**131**

Introduction

Welcome to Vietnam

Overview of Vietnam

Imagine a land where ancient traditions meld seamlessly with the rush of modern life. Vietnam, located in Southeast Asia, is just that place. This S-shaped wonder spans over 3,000 kilometers of coastline, offering breathtaking views that range from the stunning emerald waters of Ha Long Bay to the vibrant, terraced fields of Sapa. Here, bustling cities like Hanoi and Ho Chi Minh City coexist with tranquil, picturesque villages that seem almost untouched by time.

Vietnam is a mosaic of culture, home to 54 ethnic groups, each adding its unique thread to the country's rich cultural fabric. The warmth, hospitality, and tenacity of the Vietnamese people are well-known and stem from a history marked by resilience and determination. Despite challenges, the nation has evolved into one of Asia's most dynamic economies, blending rapid modernization with its age-old heritage.

Vietnamese cuisine has earned international acclaim for its bold flavors and fresh ingredients. From the aromatic, comforting pho to the delicious, savory banh mi, the food scene here promises a culinary adventure like no other.

Why Visit Vietnam in 2025

As we step into 2025, Vietnam emerges as an unmatched destination for travelers seeking a blend of adventure and cultural immersion. Here are some compelling reasons to add Vietnam to your travel plans this year:

1. **Enhanced Tourism Infrastructure:** Vietnam has poured significant resources into improving its tourism infrastructure. With better transportation networks, modern hotels, and a wide range of tour options, exploring Vietnam has never been easier or more comfortable.

2. **Cultural Festivals and Events:** 2025 is brimming with vibrant cultural festivals and events that highlight Vietnam's rich heritage. From the Tet Nguyen Dan (Lunar New Year) celebrations to the joyful Mid-Autumn Festival, you'll have the chance to participate in traditional festivities that offer an authentic glimpse into Vietnamese culture.

3. **Natural Wonders**: Vietnam's diverse landscapes are truly mesmerizing. In 2025, new eco-tourism initiatives and conservation efforts make it possible to experience these natural wonders sustainably. Whether you're trekking through the terraced fields of Mu Cang Chai or taking a serene cruise along the Mekong Delta, Vietnam offers endless outdoor adventures.

4. **Culinary Delights:** Vietnam's cuisine is a standout for many travelers, and 2025 is set to be a feast for the senses. With the rise of farm-to-table dining and innovative fusion dishes, food enthusiasts can enjoy both traditional meals and contemporary culinary creations.

5. **Historical and Cultural Exploration**: Vietnam's history is rich and complex, with tales of ancient dynasties, colonial influences, and revolutionary heroes. In 2025, museums, historical sites, and guided tours will provide deeper insights into this captivating past, allowing you to connect with the country's cultural roots.

6. **Affordable Travel:** Despite its increasing popularity, Vietnam remains a budget-friendly destination. In 2025, you can enjoy a top-notch travel experience without breaking the bank. From affordable accommodations to reasonably priced street food, Vietnam offers excellent value for your money.

7. **Warm and Welcoming People**: The friendliness and hospitality of the Vietnamese people are legendary. As a visitor in 2025, expect to be greeted with genuine warmth and open arms, making your journey through Vietnam even more memorable.

Conclusion:

With its stunning landscapes, rich cultural heritage, and exciting developments, Vietnam promises unforgettable experiences. Whether you're an adventurer, a history enthusiast, a foodie, or simply seeking a new and enriching travel experience, Vietnam in 2025 has something for everyone. Embark on this journey and uncover the wonders that await in this enchanting country.

Quick Facts about Vietnam

Geography, Population, and Culture

Vietnam, located in Southeast Asia, boasts an incredibly diverse landscape that includes rugged mountains, fertile deltas, and pristine beaches. The country's topography ranges from the misty mountains of the north to the bustling cities and serene coastlines in the south.

With a population of over 96 million people, Vietnam is the 15th most populous country in the world. The majority of the population is concentrated in major cities such as Hanoi, the capital, and Ho Chi Minh City, the bustling economic hub. However, there are also numerous smaller towns and rural areas where traditional ways of life continue to thrive.

Vietnamese culture is a rich tapestry woven with influences from various ethnic groups, historical periods, and neighboring countries. The country is home to 54 ethnic groups, with the Kinh (or Viet) people making up about 85% of the population. Each ethnic group has its own distinct customs, traditions, and festivals, contributing to the vibrant cultural mosaic of the nation.

The Vietnamese are known for their warm hospitality, resilience, and strong sense of community. Traditional values such as respect for elders, filial piety, and the importance of family play a significant role in everyday life.

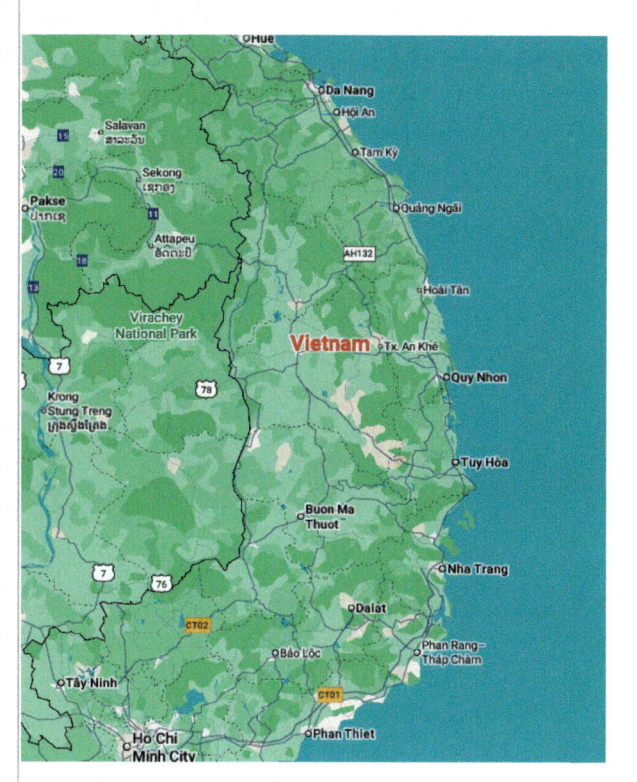

Language

The official language of Vietnam is Vietnamese, a tonal language that belongs to the Austroasiatic language family. Vietnamese is spoken by the majority of the population and serves as the primary means of communication in government, education, and media.

In addition to Vietnamese, there are several minority languages spoken by the various ethnic groups in the country. These languages include Tay, Muong, Khmer, Chinese, and Hmong, among others. In urban areas and tourist destinations, you will often find people who speak English, especially among the younger generation and those working in the tourism industry.

Currency
The official currency of Vietnam is the Vietnamese Dong (VND), which is abbreviated as "₫". Banknotes come in various denominations, ranging from 100 VND to 500,000 VND. Coins are also in circulation, though they are less commonly used.

The Vietnamese Dong is a relatively weak currency compared to major world currencies like the US Dollar or Euro, making Vietnam an affordable destination for travelers. Currency exchange services are widely available at airports, banks, hotels, and licensed exchange bureaus.

Time Zone
Vietnam operates on Indochina Time (ICT), which is 7 hours ahead of Coordinated Universal Time (UTC+7). The country does not observe daylight saving time, so the time difference remains constant throughout the year.

This time zone places Vietnam 12 hours ahead of Eastern Standard Time (EST) and 14 hours ahead of Pacific Standard Time (PST) in the United States. When planning your trip, it's essential to keep this time difference in mind to coordinate communication and activities with those in different time zones.

Chapter 1: Planning Your Trip

When to Visit Vietnam

Vietnam is a land of timeless beauty and captivating charm, where every season offers a unique opportunity to explore its rich landscapes and cultural heritage. Knowing the best times to visit can elevate your travel experience, ensuring that you encounter the country at its most enchanting.

Best Seasons to Travel

Spring (March to April):
Spring in Vietnam is a season of renewal, with mild temperatures and blooming landscapes. It's a perfect time to explore and immerse yourself in the beauty of the country.

What to Expect: Spring is marked by mild temperatures, ranging from 20°C to 30°C (68°F to 86°F), and lower humidity levels. The landscapes are lush and vibrant, making it an ideal time for sightseeing and outdoor activities.

How to Navigate:
- **Transportation**: Spring is a great time to explore cities like Hanoi and Hue. You can navigate these cities using a combination of taxis, motorbike rentals, and local buses. For longer distances, consider taking comfortable overnight trains or flights.
- **Highlights**: Enjoy leisurely walks around Hanoi's Old Quarter, visit the ancient citadel in Hue, and explore the picturesque countryside. The Perfume Pagoda Festival, held during this

season, offers a unique cultural experience with its vibrant ceremonies and scenic boat rides.

Summer (May to August):
Summer in Vietnam brings warmth and energy, perfect for those seeking adventure and beach activities. Despite the heat, there's much to enjoy if you know how to navigate it.

What to Expect: Summer brings hot and humid weather, especially in the northern and central regions, with temperatures often exceeding 35°C (95°F). Frequent rain showers are common, providing a refreshing break from the heat.

How to Navigate:
- **Transportation**: While the heat can be intense, it's a great time for beach activities and trekking. Rent a car or motorbike for flexibility and take advantage of local buses for shorter trips. Consider guided tours for trekking to ensure safety and local insights.
- **Highlights**: Head to the coastal areas like Phu Quoc and Con Dao for sun-soaked beaches and clear waters. In the northern highlands, embark on trekking adventures in Sapa, where the lush green landscapes are a sight to behold. The Danang International Fireworks Festival, held in summer, is a spectacular event that lights up the night sky.

Autumn (September to November):
Autumn paints Vietnam in golden hues, offering cool temperatures and clear skies. This season is perfect for exploring both urban and rural landscapes.

What to Expect: Autumn is characterized by cool, comfortable temperatures ranging from 25°C to 28°C (77°F to 82°F) and clear skies. The northern regions, in particular, are stunning during this time.

How to Navigate:
- **Transportation:** Autumn is perfect for exploring both urban and rural areas. Use a mix of public transportation, taxis, and motorbike rentals to get around. Train travel is also a scenic and convenient option for longer journeys.
- **Highlights**: Discover the golden terraced rice fields of Sapa and Ha Giang, perfect for photography and trekking. Explore the ancient town of Hoi An, with its lantern-lit streets and cultural heritage. Attend the Mid-Autumn Festival, where you can enjoy colorful lantern displays and delicious mooncakes.

Winter (December to February):
Winter in Vietnam is a time of contrasts, with chilly northern regions and warm southern areas. It's an ideal season for cultural experiences and southern beach getaways.

What to Expect: Winter in northern Vietnam can be chilly, with temperatures dropping to around 10°C (50°F), while the southern regions remain warm and inviting. This is the peak tourist season for places like Ho Chi Minh City and the Mekong Delta.

How to Navigate:

- **Transportation**: In the north, pack warm clothing and opt for cozy accommodations. In the south, enjoy the warm weather with light clothing. Use a combination of flights, buses, and taxis to navigate different regions. Booking accommodations and transport in advance is recommended during the busy Tet holiday.
- **Highlights**: Celebrate Tet (Lunar New Year) with the locals, experiencing traditional customs and festivities. In Ho Chi Minh City, explore the bustling markets and historical sites. The Mekong Delta offers unique experiences, such as floating markets and river cruises, perfect for a winter adventure.

I hope this revision provides a comprehensive, friendly, and professional guide on what to expect and how to navigate each season in Vietnam. If there are any specific details or personal touches you'd like to add, just let me know!

Festivals and Events

Vietnam is a country rich in cultural traditions, and its festivals and events offer a unique window into the soul of the nation. From vibrant celebrations to solemn ceremonies, each festival provides an opportunity to connect with the local culture and traditions.

Tet Nguyen Dan (Lunar New Year):
Tet, the Lunar New Year, is the most important and widely celebrated festival in Vietnam. It usually falls between late January and early February, marking the arrival of spring. During Tet, families come together to honor their ancestors, enjoy traditional foods, and participate in cultural activities.

What to Expect: The entire country comes alive with colorful decorations, bustling markets, and festive parades. Streets are adorned with kumquat trees and peach blossoms, and the air is filled with the scent of incense and traditional dishes. Expect a vibrant and joyous atmosphere as families and friends gather to celebrate the new year.

How to Navigate:
- **Planning**: Tet is a busy travel period, so it's essential to book accommodations and transportation well in advance. Many businesses close for the holiday, so plan your itinerary accordingly.
- **Participating**: Embrace the local customs by visiting temples, giving lucky money to children, and enjoying traditional foods like banh chung (square sticky rice cake) and gio lua (Vietnamese pork sausage).

Mid-Autumn Festival:
The Mid-Autumn Festival, also known as the Moon Festival, takes place in September or October. It's a time for families to gather and celebrate the harvest with mooncakes, lanterns, and lion dances.

What to Expect: Expect lively parades, colorful lantern displays, and bustling markets selling mooncakes and other treats. The streets are filled with children carrying lanterns and performing lion dances, creating a festive and joyous atmosphere.

How to Navigate:
- **Planning**: The Mid-Autumn Festival is celebrated in many cities and towns across Vietnam. Major celebrations can be found in Hanoi, Ho Chi Minh City, and Hoi An.
- **Participating**: Join in the fun by attending lantern parades, enjoying mooncakes, and watching lion dances. The festival is a family-oriented event, so it's a great time to experience the warmth and hospitality of Vietnamese families.

Hue Festival:
Held biennially in April, the Hue Festival is a grand celebration of the cultural heritage of Hue, the former imperial capital of Vietnam. The festival features traditional music and dance performances, art exhibitions, and historical reenactments.

What to Expect: Expect a vibrant showcase of Vietnam's cultural heritage with performances, exhibitions, and reenactments held in historic sites across Hue. The city's ancient citadel, royal tombs, and pagodas come alive with cultural activities and events.

How to Navigate:
- **Planning**: The Hue Festival attracts visitors from around the world, so book your accommodations early. The festival program is packed with events, so plan your itinerary to catch your favorite performances and exhibitions.
- **Participating**: Explore the historic sites of Hue, enjoy traditional performances, and participate in cultural workshops and activities. The festival offers a unique opportunity to immerse yourself in the rich history and culture of Hue.

Hanoi International Film Festival:
This biennial event, held in October or November, showcases the best of Vietnamese and international cinema. Film enthusiasts can enjoy screenings, workshops, and discussions with filmmakers from around the world.

What to Expect: Expect a diverse selection of films, from Vietnamese cinema to international releases. The festival includes screenings, panel discussions, and workshops with filmmakers, offering a unique opportunity to engage with the world of cinema.

How to Navigate:
- **Planning**: The Hanoi International Film Festival is held in various venues across Hanoi. Check the festival program for screening times and locations, and book your tickets in advance.
- **Participating**: Attend screenings of your favorite films, join panel discussions with filmmakers, and participate in workshops to learn more about the art of filmmaking. The festival is a great way to experience the vibrant film culture of Vietnam.

Weather Patterns
Understanding Vietnam's weather patterns is essential for planning your trip, as the climate varies significantly from north to south. Here's

a detailed look at what to expect in different regions and how to navigate the diverse weather conditions, along with some personal experiences to make it more engaging.

Northern Vietnam:
Northern Vietnam experiences four distinct seasons, each offering a unique charm.

Spring (March to April):
In the north, spring brings mild temperatures ranging from 15°C to 25°C (59°F to 77°F). The landscapes are lush and green, perfect for exploring Hanoi, Ha Long Bay, and the terraced fields of Sapa. Light clothing with a light jacket for cooler evenings is recommended.

Personal Experience: I remember walking around Hanoi's Old Quarter during a beautiful spring afternoon. The streets were adorned with blossoming flowers, and the air was filled with the aroma of freshly brewed coffee. The gentle breeze made the stroll incredibly pleasant, and I spent hours exploring the local markets and quaint cafes.

Summer (May to August):
Summer in northern Vietnam is hot and humid, with temperatures often exceeding 30°C (86°F). Frequent rain showers are common, providing a refreshing break from the heat. It's an excellent time for trekking in the highlands and enjoying the vibrant outdoor markets. Light, breathable clothing and rain gear are essential.

Personal Experience: Trekking in Sapa during the summer was an adventure I'll never forget. The lush, green terraces stretched as far as the eye could see, and the occasional rain showers added a refreshing touch to the journey. The local H'mong people were incredibly welcoming, and I had the chance to learn about their traditional way of life.

Autumn (September to November):
Autumn is a favorite season for many travelers, with temperatures ranging from 20°C to 28°C (68°F to 82°F). The skies are clear, and the air is crisp. This is the best time to visit Ha Long Bay for crystal-clear views and to explore the golden terraced fields of Sapa. Layered clothing is ideal for varying temperatures.

Personal Experience: Cruising through Ha Long Bay in the autumn was like a dream. The emerald waters reflected the clear blue skies, and the limestone karsts stood majestically in the distance. The cool breeze made it the perfect time to relax on the deck and take in the stunning views.

Winter (December to February):
Winter in the north can be chilly, especially in the mountains, with temperatures dropping to 10°C (50°F) or lower. Hanoi and surrounding areas experience cooler weather, making it a great time for cultural exploration. Warm clothing, including sweaters and jackets, is necessary.

Personal Experience: Visiting Hanoi during the winter was a unique experience. The cool weather added a cozy charm to the city, and I enjoyed sipping on hot pho at a street-side eatery. The Tet (Lunar New Year) celebrations were in full swing, and the city's vibrant decorations and festive spirit were unforgettable.

Central Vietnam:
Central Vietnam has a tropical monsoon climate with distinct wet and dry seasons.

Dry Season (January to August):
The dry season in central Vietnam offers warm and sunny weather, with temperatures ranging from 25°C to 35°C (77°F to 95°F). This is the perfect time to visit the historic town of Hoi An, the imperial city of Hue, and the coastal city of Da Nang. Light, comfortable clothing and sun protection are essential.

Personal Experience: Strolling through the lantern-lit streets of Hoi An during the dry season felt like stepping back in time. The ancient architecture, combined with the warm glow of the lanterns, created a magical atmosphere. I also enjoyed a peaceful boat ride along the Thu Bon River, taking in the picturesque views.

Rainy Season (September to December):
The rainy season brings frequent showers and occasional typhoons, especially in October and November. While the rain can be heavy, it doesn't last all day. Visiting during this time allows you to experience the lush green landscapes and fewer crowds. Waterproof clothing and footwear are recommended.

Personal Experience: Exploring Hue during the rainy season had its own charm. The rain added a serene beauty to the ancient citadel, and I spent hours wandering through the historical sites. The fewer crowds allowed for a more intimate experience, and the local cuisine was heartwarming on a rainy day.

Southern Vietnam:
Southern Vietnam enjoys a tropical climate with two main seasons: dry and rainy.

Dry Season (December to April):
The dry season in the south is characterized by warm temperatures, averaging around 27°C (81°F), and low humidity. This is the best time to explore Ho Chi Minh City, the Mekong Delta, and the pristine beaches of Phu Quoc. Light, breathable clothing and sun protection are necessary.

Personal Experience: Basking in the sun on the beaches of Phu Quoc during the dry season was pure bliss. The crystal-clear waters and soft sandy beaches were perfect for relaxation. I also took a trip to the Mekong Delta, where I enjoyed a boat ride through the winding waterways, surrounded by lush greenery.

Rainy Season (May to November):
The rainy season brings daily showers, usually in the afternoon, with temperatures remaining warm. The rains make the landscapes lush and vibrant, perfect for exploring the natural beauty of the Mekong Delta. Waterproof gear and an umbrella are essential for navigating the rain.

Personal Experience: Visiting the Mekong Delta during the rainy season was an adventure. The afternoon showers added a refreshing touch to the lush landscapes, and I enjoyed exploring the floating markets. The local vendors were friendly, and I savored the fresh tropical fruits and delicious Vietnamese dishes.

Understanding these weather patterns and personal experiences will help you plan your wardrobe and activities, ensuring a comfortable and enjoyable trip. Whether you're trekking through the northern highlands, exploring historic sites in the central region, or relaxing on southern beaches, Vietnam's diverse climate offers something for every traveler.

Visa and Entry Requirements

Navigating the visa and entry requirements for Vietnam can seem daunting, but with the right information, the process becomes smooth and straightforward. Let's dive into the details, making it easy for you to plan your adventure.

Types of Visas

Vietnam offers several types of visas to cater to different travel needs. Understanding the options will help you choose the right one for your journey.

Tourist Visa (DL): The most common type for travelers, the tourist visa allows you to explore Vietnam for up to 30 days. It can be extended once for an additional 30 days without leaving the country.

Personal Experience: During my first visit to Vietnam, I opted for the tourist visa. The initial 30 days were perfect for a whirlwind tour of Hanoi, Ha Long Bay, and Hoi An. Extending the visa for another month allowed me to delve deeper into the culture and explore off-the-beaten-path destinations.

Business Visa (DN): For those traveling for work or business meetings, the business visa grants a stay of up to 12 months. It's available in single-entry and multiple-entry options.

Student Visa (DH): If you're planning to study in Vietnam, the student visa is your go-to option. It's usually arranged by the educational institution and is valid for the duration of your course.

Work Visa (LD): For employment in Vietnam, the work visa is essential. Employers typically sponsor this visa, and it's valid for up to two years.

Transit Visa: For travelers passing through Vietnam on their way to another destination, the transit visa allows a short stay of up to 5 days.

Understanding the types of visas available will help you select the one that best suits your travel plans. Whether you're visiting for leisure, business, or study, Vietnam has a visa option to accommodate your needs. Next, let's move on to the application process.

Application Process

Tourist Visa (DL):

Online Application (e-Visa):
Steps:
1. Fill out the application form on the official Vietnam e-Visa website with your personal details and travel information.
2. Upload a recent passport-sized photo and a scanned copy of your passport.

3. Pay the processing fee of $25 for a single-entry visa using a credit or debit card.
4. Once approved, you will receive your e-Visa via email. Print a copy to present upon arrival.

Important Tips:
- Ensure your passport is valid for at least six months beyond your intended stay.
- Double-check all details before submission to avoid any errors.
- Keep a printed copy of your e-Visa and entry-exit form for arrival.

Visa on Arrival (VOA):
Steps:
1. Obtain a visa approval letter through a reputable travel agency before your trip.
2. Upon arrival at a Vietnamese airport, present the approval letter, completed entry-exit form, passport, and passport-sized photos at the VOA counter.
3. Pay the stamping fee of $25 for a single-entry visa or $50 for a multiple-entry visa and receive your visa.

Important Tips:
- Make sure the approval letter is from a trusted agency to avoid any issues.
- Bring multiple copies of your passport-sized photos.
- Have cash in USD for the stamping fee to expedite the process.

Embassy/Consulate Application:
Steps:
1. Visit the nearest Vietnamese embassy or consulate with your passport, completed application form, passport-sized photos, and the visa fee.
2. Submit the documents and wait for processing.

Important Tips:
- Check the specific requirements and processing times with the embassy or consulate.
- Plan ahead, as processing times can vary.

Business Visa (DN):
Online Application:
Steps:
1. Obtain an invitation letter from a Vietnamese business partner or employer.
2. Apply online for an e-Visa using the same steps as the tourist e-Visa.

Important Tips:
- Ensure the invitation letter includes all necessary details, such as your name, passport number, and travel dates.

Embassy/Consulate Application:
Steps:
1. Visit the nearest Vietnamese embassy or consulate with your invitation letter, passport, completed application form, passport-sized photos, and the visa fee.
2. Submit the documents and wait for processing.

Important Tips:
- Contact the embassy or consulate for specific requirements and processing times.
- Plan for potential delays, especially during peak travel periods.

Student Visa (DH):
Steps:
1. Obtain an acceptance letter from the Vietnamese educational institution where you will be studying.

2. The educational institution will assist you with the visa application process, including submitting your passport, completed application form, and passport-sized photos to the immigration authorities.

3. Wait for processing and receive your visa.

Important Tips:
- Apply well in advance of your course start date to avoid any delays.
- Keep all communication with the educational institution for reference.

Work Visa (LD):

Steps:

1. Secure a job offer from a Vietnamese employer who will sponsor your work visa.

2. Obtain a work permit with the assistance of your employer.

3. Apply for the work visa at the nearest Vietnamese embassy or consulate with your passport, completed application form, passport-sized photos, work permit, and the visa fee.

Important Tips:
- Ensure all documents are complete and accurate to avoid delays.
- Keep in regular contact with your employer throughout the application process.

Transit Visa:

Steps:

1. Provide proof of onward travel, such as a flight ticket to your final destination.

2. Apply for the transit visa at the nearest Vietnamese embassy or consulate with your passport, completed application form, passport-sized photos, and the visa fee.

Important Tips:
- Plan your transit time to allow for any unexpected delays.
- Have all necessary documents readily accessible for inspection.

Custom Regulations

When entering Vietnam, it's important to be aware of the customs regulations to ensure a smooth arrival.

- **Prohibited Items:** Certain items are prohibited from being brought into Vietnam, including narcotics, explosives, and firearms. Additionally, culturally sensitive materials and certain medications may be restricted.
- **Duty-Free Allowance**: Travelers are allowed to bring a limited quantity of duty-free items into Vietnam, including alcohol, tobacco, and personal items. Check the specific allowances to avoid any issues at customs.
- **Declaration Forms**: If you are carrying large amounts of cash (over USD 5,000) or valuable items, you must declare them upon entry. Be sure to fill out the customs declaration form accurately.

Personal Experience: Upon arrival in Vietnam, I found the customs process to be efficient. Having my documents organized and knowing the regulations in advance made the experience smooth. The customs officers were friendly, and I was quickly on my way to enjoy my adventure.

When entering Vietnam, it's essential to be aware of the customs regulations to ensure a smooth and hassle-free arrival. Understanding the rules and procedures will help you avoid any complications and make your entry into the country seamless. Here's a comprehensive guide to Vietnam's custom regulations.

Prohibited and Restricted Items

Vietnam has strict regulations on certain items that are either prohibited or restricted from being brought into the country. Being aware of these regulations will help you avoid any legal issues at the border.

Prohibited Items:

- **Narcotics and illegal drugs**: Bringing narcotics into Vietnam is strictly prohibited and can result in severe legal consequences, including imprisonment.
- **Explosives and firearms**: Importing explosives, firearms, and ammunition is not allowed unless you have special permission from the relevant authorities.
- **Culturally sensitive materials:** Items that are considered offensive or harmful to Vietnamese culture, such as pornographic materials, anti-government propaganda, and documents promoting discrimination or hatred, are prohibited.
- **Counterfeit goods:** Importing counterfeit currency, goods, and documents is illegal and subject to confiscation and fines.

Restricted Items:

- **Medications**: Certain medications, especially those containing narcotic substances, require a prescription and prior approval from the Vietnamese Ministry of Health. It's advisable to carry a copy of your prescription and a doctor's note explaining the necessity of the medication.
- **Endangered species:** Importing products made from endangered species, such as ivory, rhino horn, and certain animal skins, is restricted and requires special permits.
- **High-value electronics**: High-value electronics, such as drones and professional camera equipment, may be subject to inspection and declaration upon entry.

Duty-Free Allowance

Travelers entering Vietnam are allowed to bring a limited quantity of duty-free items into the country. Exceeding these allowances may result in additional duties and taxes.

Alcohol:
- Up to 1.5 liters of spirits (over 22% alcohol content) or 2 liters of wine (under 22% alcohol content) or 3 liters of beer.

Tobacco:
Up to 200 cigarettes or 100 cigars or 500 grams of tobacco.

Personal Items:
- Reasonable quantities of personal items for personal use, such as clothing, toiletries, and personal electronics, are allowed duty-free.

Gifts and Souvenirs:
- Gifts and souvenirs valued up to USD 300 are allowed duty-free.

Declaration Forms

When entering Vietnam, travelers are required to fill out a customs declaration form if they are carrying certain items or amounts of cash. Accurate and honest completion of the form is crucial to avoid any issues.

Cash:
- If you are carrying cash or valuable items worth more than USD 5,000, you must declare them upon entry. Failure to do so may result in confiscation or fines.
- Valuable Items:
- Declare high-value items such as jewelry, watches, and electronics to avoid any disputes upon exit regarding their origin and ownership.

Firearms and Ammunition:
- As mentioned, firearms and ammunition require special permits and must be declared.

Tips for a Smooth Customs Experience

To ensure a smooth and efficient customs experience upon arrival in Vietnam, keep the following tips in mind:

1. **Organize Your Documents:**
   - Keep all essential documents, such as your passport, visa, customs declaration form, and any necessary permits, readily accessible.
2. **Be Honest and Accurate:**
   - Fill out the customs declaration form accurately and honestly. Provide clear and truthful information about the items you are carrying.
3. **Follow Instructions:**
   - Follow the instructions given by customs officers and cooperate with any inspections or requests for additional information.
4. **Stay Informed:**
   - Stay informed about the latest customs regulations and updates by checking the official Vietnamese customs website or consulting with your airline or travel agent.
5. **Respect Local Laws:**
   - Respect Vietnamese customs regulations and local laws. Avoid bringing prohibited items and ensure that any restricted items are properly declared and permitted.

Personal Experience: During my travels to Vietnam, I found the customs process to be efficient and straightforward. Having my documents organized and understanding the regulations in advance made the experience smooth. The customs officers were professional and courteous, and I was quickly on my way to start my adventure.

Getting There

Traveling to Vietnam is an exciting journey, and knowing how to get there is the first step to ensuring a smooth and enjoyable experience. Whether you're arriving by air or crossing the border by land, here's a comprehensive guide to help you navigate the major international airports, airlines, and border crossings in Vietnam.

Major International Airports

Vietnam is well-connected to the world through several major international airports, making it easy for travelers to reach this beautiful country. Let's explore the key international airports, what to expect, and how to navigate them:

Noi Bai International Airport (HAN) - Hanoi:

Located about 27 kilometers from downtown Hanoi, Noi Bai International Airport is the main gateway to northern Vietnam. The airport features two terminals: T1 for domestic flights and T2 for international flights.

Highlights:
- Modern facilities including free WiFi, currency exchange centers, duty-free shops, and dining options.
- Efficient immigration and customs procedures.
- Easy access to Hanoi city center via taxi, shuttle bus, or ride-sharing services.

What to Expect:
- Smooth immigration and customs process.
- A range of amenities to make your arrival comfortable.

How to Navigate:
- Follow the signs to the immigration counters for passport control.
- Collect your baggage from the designated carousel and proceed through customs.
- Head to the arrivals hall where you can find transportation options to the city.

Tan Son Nhat International Airport (SGN) - Ho Chi Minh City:

As the busiest airport in Vietnam, Tan Son Nhat International Airport serves as the primary entry point for travelers heading to southern Vietnam. It is situated just 7 kilometers from the city center.

Highlights:
- Modern amenities including lounges, restaurants, and shopping outlets.
- Quick access to Ho Chi Minh City's attractions.
1. Various transportation options including taxis, buses, and ride-sharing services.

What to Expect:
- Efficient handling of international and domestic flights.
- A bustling airport environment with numerous facilities.

How to Navigate:
- Proceed to the immigration counters for passport control upon arrival.
- Collect your luggage and pass through customs.
- In the arrivals area, find transportation options to the city, such as taxis or shuttle buses.

Da Nang International Airport (DAD) - Da Nang:

Located in central Vietnam, Da Nang International Airport is the third-largest airport in the country. It serves as a gateway to popular destinations like Hoi An and Hue.

Highlights:
- Efficient services and modern facilities including free WiFi, ATMs, and dining options.
- Easy access to Da Nang city center and nearby attractions.
- Close proximity to coastal areas and historic sites.

What to Expect:
- A smaller, less crowded airport compared to Hanoi and Ho Chi Minh City.
- Friendly and helpful airport staff.

How to Navigate:
- Complete immigration procedures and collect your baggage.
- Proceed through customs and enter the arrivals hall.
- Choose from various transportation options, including taxis and shuttle buses, to reach your destination.

Cam Ranh International Airport (CXR) - Nha Trang:
Situated in Khanh Hoa province, Cam Ranh International Airport is the main airport for travelers visiting the coastal city of Nha Trang.

Highlights:
- Duty-free shops, restaurants, and car rental facilities.
- Proximity to Nha Trang's beaches and resorts.
- Modern terminal with various amenities.

What to Expect:
- A relaxing arrival experience with fewer crowds.
- Quick access to Nha Trang's coastal attractions.

How to Navigate:
- Follow the signs to immigration and customs.
- Collect your luggage and proceed to the arrivals hall.
- Find transportation options such as taxis or shuttle services to reach your accommodation.

Phu Quoc International Airport (PQC) - Phu Quoc:
Located on Phu Quoc Island, this airport is the primary entry point for visitors to the island's stunning beaches and resorts.

Highlights:
- Modern amenities including free WiFi, currency exchange, and dining options.
- Quick access to Phu Quoc's beach resorts.
- Convenient transportation options including taxis and shuttle services.

What to Expect:
- A smooth arrival experience with modern facilities.
- Easy access to the island's attractions.

How to Navigate:
- Complete immigration and customs procedures.
- Collect your baggage and head to the arrivals area.
- Choose from various transportation options to reach your hotel or resort.

Airlines and Flights
Vietnam is served by a variety of international airlines, making it easy to find flights that suit your preferences and budget. Here are some of the top airlines that fly to Vietnam, their highlights, what to expect, and pricing information:

Vietnam Airlines:
As the national flag carrier, Vietnam Airlines offers a blend of traditional Vietnamese hospitality and modern aviation technology. The airline operates flights to major cities worldwide, including direct flights from the U.S. to Ho Chi Minh City.

Highlights:
- In-flight meals featuring Vietnamese cuisine.
- Comfortable seating with modern amenities.
- Friendly and professional cabin crew.

What to Expect:
- High-quality service and punctual flights.
- A taste of Vietnamese culture on board.

Pricing:
- Economy class fares typically range from $600 to $1,200 for round-trip flights from major cities like New York and Los Angeles to Ho Chi Minh City.
- Business class fares range from $2,000 to $3,500.

Qatar Airways:
Known for its excellent service and comfortable flights, Qatar Airways connects Vietnam with major cities in Europe, the Middle East, and the Americas.

Highlights:
- Award-winning service and comfortable cabins.
- Extensive in-flight entertainment options.
- Convenient connections through Doha.

What to Expect:
- A luxurious travel experience with spacious seating.
- High-quality in-flight meals and amenities.

Pricing:
- Economy class fares typically range from $700 to $1,400 for round-trip flights from cities like London and Paris to Hanoi.
- Business class fares range from $2,500 to $4,000.

Singapore Airlines:
Renowned for its top-notch service, Singapore Airlines operates flights to Vietnam from various cities around the world, with convenient connections through its hub in Singapore.

Highlights:
- Impeccable service and comfortable seating.
- Wide range of in-flight entertainment options.
- Smooth connections through Changi Airport.

What to Expect:
- Excellent service and attention to detail.
- Comfortable and enjoyable flights.

Pricing:
- Economy class fares typically range from $650 to $1,300 for round-trip

flights from cities like Sydney and Tokyo to Ho Chi Minh City.
- Business class fares range from $2,200 to $3,800.

Cathay Pacific:
Based in Hong Kong, Cathay Pacific offers flights to Vietnam with connections to major cities in Asia, Europe, and North America.

Highlights:
- Comfortable cabins and friendly service.
- Extensive in-flight entertainment options.
- Convenient connections through Hong Kong.

What to Expect:
- A pleasant travel experience with attentive service.
- High-quality amenities and entertainment.

Pricing:
- Economy class fares typically range from $600 to $1,200 for round-trip flights from cities like San Francisco and Vancouver to Hanoi.
- Business class fares range from $2,000 to $3,500.

Emirates:
Emirates connects Vietnam with destinations across the globe through its hub in Dubai. The airline offers a luxurious travel experience with spacious cabins, gourmet meals, and a wide range of entertainment options.

Highlights:
- Luxurious cabins and high-quality service.
- Extensive entertainment options and in-flight meals.
- Convenient connections through Dubai.

What to Expect:
- A premium travel experience with top-notch amenities.
- Comfortable and enjoyable flights.

Pricing:
- Economy class fares typically range from $750 to $1,500 for round-trip flights from cities like New York and London to Ho Chi Minh City.
- Business class fares range from $2,800 to $4,500.

Entry Points and Border Crossings

Vietnam shares land borders with China, Laos, and Cambodia, providing multiple entry points for travelers arriving by land. Here are some of the key border crossings, what to expect, and how to navigate them:

China-Vietnam Border:

Mong Cai (Quang Ninh): This border crossing connects Mong Cai in Vietnam with Dongxing in China. It's a popular entry point for travelers heading to Ha Long Bay.
Highlights: Scenic route with picturesque landscapes.

What to Expect: Efficient border procedures and friendly border staff.

How to Navigate: Ensure you have the necessary visa and documents. Use buses or taxis to reach the crossing point.

Huu Nghi (Lang Son): Located near Lang Son, this crossing connects with Pingxiang in China. It's a convenient entry point for travelers heading to Hanoi.
Highlights: Historic significance and cultural sites.

What to Expect: Smooth border crossing with clear signage.

How to Navigate: Plan your transportation in advance and have your documents ready.

Laos-Vietnam Border:

Tay Trang (Dien Bien): This crossing connects Dien Bien Phu in Vietnam with Muang Khoua in Laos. It's a scenic route for travelers exploring northern Vietnam.
Highlights: Beautiful mountainous landscapes.

What to Expect: Friendly border staff and efficient procedures.

How to Navigate: Use buses or private cars for a comfortable journey. Ensure you have the required visas.

Lao Bao (Quang Tri): Connecting Quang Tri in Vietnam with Savannakhet in Laos, this crossing is popular among travelers heading to central Vietnam.
Highlights: Cultural experiences and local markets.

What to Expect: Busy border crossing with well-organized procedures.

How to Navigate: Plan your transportation and have your documents ready. Use buses or taxis to reach the crossing point.

Cambodia-Vietnam Border:

Moc Bai (Tay Ninh): This crossing connects Tay Ninh in Vietnam with Bavet in Cambodia. It's a major entry point for travelers heading to Ho Chi Minh City.
Highlights: Bustling border town with local markets.

What to Expect: Busy crossing with clear procedures.

How to Navigate: Have your visa and documents ready. Use buses or private cars for a smooth journey.

Ha Tien (Kien Giang): Located near the coast, this crossing connects Ha Tien in Vietnam with Kampot in Cambodia. It's a convenient entry point for travelers visiting the Mekong Delta and Phu Quoc Island.
Highlights: Scenic coastal route with picturesque views.

What to Expect: Efficient border procedures and friendly staff.
How to Navigate: Plan your transportation in advance. Use buses or taxis to reach the crossing point.

Important Tips:

- **Visa Requirements**: Ensure you have the appropriate visa for your entry point. Some border crossings may require specific visas or permits.
- **Transportation**: Plan your transportation in advance, whether you're traveling by bus, car, or motorbike. Check the availability of public transport and the condition of the roads.
- **Customs Regulations**: Be aware of the customs regulations for each entry point. Declare any valuable items and ensure you have the necessary documentation for your belongings.

Travel Insurance

When planning your trip to Vietnam, one of the most important considerations is securing travel insurance. Travel insurance provides peace of mind and financial protection against unexpected events that may disrupt your journey. Let's explore the importance of travel insurance and why it's a crucial component of your travel plans.

Importance of Travel Insurance

Travel insurance is an essential safeguard that offers coverage for various unforeseen circumstances. Whether you're embarking on a short vacation or an extended adventure, travel insurance can help mitigate the risks associated with travel. Here are several reasons why travel insurance is important:

1. **Medical Emergencies:** While traveling, you may encounter unexpected health issues or accidents. Travel insurance provides coverage for medical expenses, including hospitalization, doctor's visits, and medication. It also offers emergency medical evacuation if you need to be transported to a medical facility for specialized treatment.

Personal Experience: During a trip to Vietnam, a friend of mine experienced severe food poisoning and needed immediate medical attention. Thankfully, their travel insurance covered the medical expenses and ensured they received proper care without financial stress.

2. **Trip Cancellation and Interruption:** Life is unpredictable, and sometimes you may need to cancel or cut short your trip due to unforeseen events such as illness, family emergencies, or natural disasters. Travel insurance reimburses you for non-refundable expenses like flights, accommodations, and tours, helping you recover the costs of your interrupted plans.

Personal Experience: I once had to cancel a trip to Vietnam due to a family emergency. Having travel insurance meant that I could claim a refund for my non-refundable flight and hotel bookings, easing the financial burden during a stressful time.

3. **Lost or Delayed Baggage**: Losing your luggage or experiencing delayed baggage can be a major inconvenience while traveling. Travel insurance provides compensation for lost, stolen, or delayed baggage, allowing you to replace essential items and continue your journey with minimal disruption.

Personal Experience: On one of my trips to Vietnam, my checked baggage was delayed by several days. My travel insurance covered the cost of purchasing essential clothing and toiletries, making the wait for my luggage more manageable.

4. **Travel Delays**: Flight delays and cancellations are common occurrences that can disrupt your travel plans. Travel insurance compensates you for additional expenses incurred due to travel delays, such as accommodation, meals, and transportation.

Personal Experience: During a trip to Ho Chi Minh City, my connecting flight was canceled due to bad weather. My travel insurance covered the cost of an overnight hotel stay and meals, ensuring I was comfortable while waiting for the next available flight.

5. **Personal Liability:** Travel insurance often includes personal liability coverage, protecting you against legal expenses if you accidentally cause injury or damage to someone else's property while traveling.

6. **Adventure and Sports Coverage:** Vietnam offers a range of adventure activities, such as trekking, scuba diving, and motorbiking. Travel insurance can provide coverage for accidents and injuries related to these activities, ensuring you can enjoy your adventures with confidence.

7. **Peace of Mind**: Travel insurance offers peace of mind, knowing that you have a safety net in place to handle unexpected situations. It allows you to focus on enjoying your trip without worrying about potential financial setbacks.

Important Tips for Choosing Travel Insurance:

- **Coverage**: Ensure the policy covers medical emergencies, trip cancellation, baggage loss, and personal liability. Consider additional coverage for adventure activities if you plan to engage in them.
- **Policy Limits**: Check the policy limits and make sure they are sufficient for your needs.
- **Exclusions**: Be aware of any exclusions and understand what is not covered by the policy.
- **Pre-Existing Conditions**: If you have pre-existing medical conditions, check whether they are covered by the policy or if you need to purchase additional coverage.
- **Provider Reputation**: Choose a reputable insurance provider with positive reviews and a strong track record of handling claims efficiently.

Securing travel insurance is a crucial step in your travel planning process. It provides financial protection and peace of mind, allowing you to embark on your journey to Vietnam with confidence and security.

Chapter 2: Exploring Vietnam

Top Destinations

Vietnam is a country of diverse landscapes, rich history, and vibrant culture. Here are some of the top destinations that you must visit during your trip to Vietnam, including their descriptions, highlights, and what to do in each place.

Hanoi

Description: Hanoi, the capital city of Vietnam, is a blend of ancient traditions and modern development. The city is known for its well-preserved colonial architecture, bustling street markets, and serene lakes. Hanoi's historic Old Quarter is a maze of narrow streets filled with vendors, cafes, and shops.

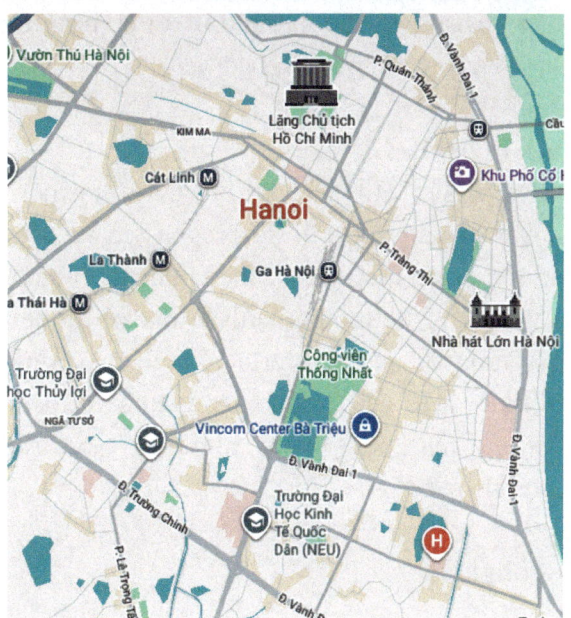

Highlights:

- **Hoan Kiem Lake:** A tranquil oasis in the heart of the city, perfect for a leisurely stroll.
- **Ho Chi Minh Mausoleum:** A significant historical site where the preserved body of President Ho Chi Minh is displayed.
- **Temple of Literature:** Vietnam's first national university, dedicated to Confucius and scholars.
- **Old Quarter:** A bustling area with narrow streets, traditional shops, and street food vendors.

What to Do:
- Explore the Old Quarter and try local delicacies like pho, banh mi, and egg coffee.
- Visit the Ho Chi Minh Mausoleum and learn about the history of Vietnam's revolutionary leader.
- Take a cyclo ride around Hoan Kiem Lake and watch the locals practice tai chi in the early morning.
- Discover the Temple of Literature and enjoy the peaceful gardens.

Ho Chi Minh City
Description: Ho Chi Minh City, formerly known as Saigon, is the largest city in Vietnam and the economic hub of the country. The city is a vibrant metropolis with a mix of modern skyscrapers and historic French colonial buildings. Ho Chi Minh City is known for its bustling markets, lively nightlife, and rich cultural scene.

Highlights:
- **Ben Thanh Market:** A bustling market where you can find everything from souvenirs to local cuisine.
- **Notre-Dame Cathedral Basilica of Saigon**: A stunning French colonial-era cathedral.
- **War Remnants Museum**: A museum documenting the Vietnam War from the Vietnamese perspective.
- **Bitexco Financial Tower:** A modern skyscraper with an observation deck offering panoramic views of the city.

What to Do:
- Shop for souvenirs and sample street food at Ben Thanh Market.
- Visit the War Remnants Museum to gain insight into Vietnam's recent history.
- Explore the historic Notre-Dame Cathedral and the Saigon Central Post Office.
- Enjoy the city's nightlife and dine at rooftop bars with views of the skyline.

Hoi An
Description: Hoi An is a charming ancient town located along the central coast of Vietnam. Known for its well-preserved architecture, lantern-lit streets, and vibrant cultural heritage, Hoi An is a UNESCO World Heritage Site. The town's riverside setting and colorful buildings create a picturesque atmosphere.

Highlights:
- **Hoi An Ancient Town:** A beautifully preserved area with historic houses, temples, and shops.

- **Japanese Covered Bridge**: An iconic symbol of Hoi An, built in the 16th century.
- **An Bang Beach**: A pristine beach just a short bike ride from the town center.
- **Hoi An Lantern Festival**: A monthly event where the town is illuminated with colorful lanterns.

What to Do:
- Wander through the ancient town and admire the well-preserved buildings.
- Cross the Japanese Covered Bridge and explore the nearby markets.
- Relax on An Bang Beach and enjoy the sun and sea.
- Visit during the Lantern Festival and experience the magical atmosphere as the town lights up with lanterns.

Da Nang

Description: Da Nang is a coastal city in central Vietnam known for its sandy beaches, modern bridges, and vibrant nightlife. The city serves as a gateway to the historic sites of Hoi An and Hue. Da Nang's natural beauty and cultural attractions make it a popular destination for travelers.

Highlights:
- **My Khe Beach**: A stunning beach known for its soft white sand and clear blue water.
- **Dragon Bridge**: A unique bridge shaped like a dragon, which lights up and breathes fire on weekends.
- **Marble Mountains**: A cluster of limestone hills with caves, temples, and panoramic views.
- **Ba Na Hills**: A mountain resort with a famous Golden Bridge held up by giant stone hands.

What to Do:
- Spend a day relaxing on My Khe Beach and enjoy water activities like surfing and paddleboarding.
- Visit the Marble Mountains and explore the caves and temples.
- Walk across the Dragon Bridge and catch the fire-breathing show in the evening.
- Take a cable car ride to Ba Na Hills and marvel at the Golden Bridge.

Each of these top destinations in Vietnam offers unique experiences, rich history, and vibrant culture. Whether you're exploring ancient streets, relaxing on pristine beaches, or immersing yourself in local traditions, Vietnam's diverse destinations promise unforgettable memories.

Itineraries

Planning your trip to Vietnam can be an exciting endeavor, and having a well-organized itinerary can help you make the most of your time in this beautiful country. From the bustling cities to the serene countryside and stunning beaches, Vietnam offers a diverse range of experiences for every traveler. Whether you have a week, ten days, or two weeks to explore, here are some suggested itineraries to guide you through the top destinations and activities in Vietnam. Each itinerary is designed to provide a balanced mix of cultural exploration, adventure, and relaxation, ensuring that you have an unforgettable journey through this captivating country.

7-Day Itinerary

Day 1: Arrival in Hanoi
- **Morning**: Arrive in Hanoi and check into your hotel.
- **Afternoon**: Explore the Old Quarter, where you can wander through narrow streets filled with vendors, cafes, and shops. Try local delicacies like pho and banh mi.
- **Evening**: Visit Hoan Kiem Lake, take a leisurely walk around the lake, and visit Ngoc Son Temple. Enjoy a traditional water puppet show.

Day 2: Hanoi
- **Morning**: Tour the Ho Chi Minh Mausoleum and learn about the history of Vietnam's revolutionary leader. Visit the Presidential Palace and One Pillar Pagoda nearby.
- **Afternoon**: Discover the Temple of Literature, Vietnam's first national university, and enjoy the peaceful gardens.
- **Evening**: Explore Hanoi's street food scene in the Old Quarter and sample dishes like bun cha and egg coffee.

Day 3: Hanoi to Ha Long Bay
- **Morning**: Depart from Hanoi and take a scenic drive to Ha Long Bay.
- **Afternoon**: Board a cruise and explore the stunning limestone karsts and emerald waters of Ha Long Bay. Visit caves and floating villages.
- **Evening**: Enjoy dinner on the cruise and relax under the stars.

Day 4: Ha Long Bay
- **Morning**: Continue cruising through Ha Long Bay, go kayaking, and swim in the clear waters.
- **Afternoon**: Return to the mainland and transfer back to Hanoi.
- **Evening**: Spend your last evening in Hanoi, exploring any sights you may have missed.

Day 5: Hanoi to Hoi An
- **Morning**: Fly from Hanoi to Da Nang and transfer to Hoi An.
- **Afternoon**: Wander through Hoi An Ancient Town, visiting historic houses, temples, and the Japanese Covered Bridge.
- **Evening**: Enjoy the vibrant atmosphere of Hoi An and dine at a riverside restaurant.

Day 6: Hoi An
- **Morning**: Relax on An Bang Beach, soaking up the sun and enjoying the crystal-clear waters.
- **Afternoon**: Explore the local markets and take a traditional cooking class to learn how to make Vietnamese dishes.
- **Evening**: Experience the Hoi An Lantern Festival if your visit coincides with the event, and enjoy the magical atmosphere as the town lights up with lanterns.

Day 7: Departure from Hoi An
- **Morning**: Spend your last morning in Hoi An, exploring any sights you may have missed or doing some last-minute shopping.

- **Afternoon**: Transfer to Da Nang Airport for your departure flight.

10-Day Itinerary

Planning a 10-day trip to Vietnam offers a perfect balance of cultural exploration, natural beauty, and relaxation. Here's a detailed itinerary to help you make the most of your visit to this captivating country.

Day 1: Arrival in Hanoi
- **Morning**: Arrive in Hanoi and check into your hotel. Take some time to rest and refresh after your journey.
- **Afternoon**: Explore the Old Quarter, where you can wander through narrow streets filled with vendors, cafes, and shops. Try local delicacies like pho and banh mi.
- **Evening**: Visit Hoan Kiem Lake, take a leisurely walk around the lake, and visit Ngoc Son Temple. Enjoy a traditional water puppet show at the Thang Long Water Puppet Theatre.

Personal Experience: During my visit to Hanoi, I was captivated by the charm of the Old Quarter. Strolling through the bustling streets, I indulged in delicious street food and discovered hidden gems in the local markets. The highlight of my trip was visiting Hoan Kiem Lake and watching the traditional water puppet show, which was both entertaining and culturally enriching.

Day 2: Hanoi
- **Morning:** Tour the Ho Chi Minh Mausoleum and learn about the history of Vietnam's revolutionary leader. Visit the Presidential Palace and One Pillar Pagoda nearby.
- **Afternoon**: Discover the Temple of Literature, Vietnam's first national university, and enjoy the peaceful gardens. Visit the Vietnam Museum of Ethnology to learn about the diverse ethnic groups in Vietnam.
- **Evening**: Explore Hanoi's street food scene in the Old Quarter and sample dishes like bun cha and egg coffee.

Personal Experience: Visiting the Ho Chi Minh Mausoleum was a moving experience, and learning about the life and legacy of Ho Chi Minh provided valuable insights into Vietnam's history. The Temple of Literature was a serene escape from the city's hustle and bustle, and the Vietnam Museum of Ethnology offered a fascinating look into the country's cultural diversity.

Day 3: Hanoi to Ha Long Bay
- **Morning**: Depart from Hanoi and take a scenic drive to Ha Long Bay.
- **Afternoon**: Board a cruise and explore the stunning limestone karsts and emerald waters of Ha Long Bay. Visit caves and floating villages.
- **Evening**: Enjoy dinner on the cruise and relax under the stars.

Personal Experience: The cruise through Ha Long Bay was a highlight of my trip. The breathtaking scenery of limestone karsts rising from the emerald waters was truly mesmerizing. Visiting the caves and floating villages provided a glimpse into the local way of life, and enjoying dinner under the stars on the deck of the cruise was a magical experience.

Day 4: Ha Long Bay
- **Morning**: Continue cruising through Ha Long Bay, go kayaking, and swim in the clear waters.
- **Afternoon**: Return to the mainland and transfer back to Hanoi.
- **Evening**: Spend your last evening in Hanoi, exploring any sights you may have missed or relaxing at a local cafe.

Personal Experience: Kayaking in Ha Long Bay allowed me to explore hidden corners and get up close to the stunning rock formations. Swimming in the clear waters was refreshing, and the entire experience left me in awe of the natural beauty of the bay.

Day 5: Hanoi to Hoi An
- **Morning**: Fly from Hanoi to Da Nang and transfer to Hoi An.
- **Afternoon**: Wander through Hoi An Ancient Town, visiting historic houses, temples, and the Japanese Covered Bridge.
- **Evening**: Enjoy the vibrant atmosphere of Hoi An and dine at a riverside restaurant.

Personal Experience: Hoi An's enchanting beauty and rich history made it one of my favorite destinations in Vietnam. Wandering through the lantern-lit streets, I discovered hidden gems and indulged in delicious local cuisine. The Japanese Covered Bridge and historic houses were fascinating to explore, and dining by the riverside was a delightful experience.

Day 6: Hoi An
- **Morning**: Relax on An Bang Beach, soaking up the sun and enjoying the crystal-clear waters.
- **Afternoon**: Explore the local markets and take a traditional cooking class to learn how to make Vietnamese dishes.
- **Evening**: Experience the Hoi An Lantern Festival if your visit coincides with the event, and enjoy the magical atmosphere as the town lights up with lanterns.

Personal Experience: Relaxing on An Bang Beach was the perfect way to unwind and enjoy the natural beauty of the area. The cooking class was a highlight, as I learned how to make traditional Vietnamese dishes and gained a deeper appreciation for the country's culinary heritage. The Hoi An Lantern Festival was a magical experience, with the entire town illuminated by colorful lanterns.

Day 7: Hoi An to Da Nang
- **Morning**: Spend the morning in Hoi An, exploring any sights you may have missed.
- **Afternoon**: Transfer to Da Nang and visit the Marble Mountains, where you can explore the caves and temples and enjoy panoramic views of the city and coastline.
- **Evening**: Relax on My Khe Beach and enjoy a seafood dinner at a beachfront restaurant.

Personal Experience: The Marble Mountains were a fascinating destination, with intricate cave systems and beautiful temples to explore.

The views from the top were breathtaking, and it was a great way to spend an afternoon. Relaxing on My Khe Beach and enjoying fresh seafood while watching the sunset was a perfect end to the day.

Day 8: Travel to Ho Chi Minh City
- **Morning**: Fly from Da Nang to Ho Chi Minh City and check into your hotel.
- **Afternoon**: Visit Ben Thanh Market and explore the bustling stalls, where you can shop for souvenirs and try local street food.
- **Evening**: Dine at a rooftop bar and enjoy panoramic views of the city skyline.

Personal Experience: Ho Chi Minh City's dynamic energy and vibrant markets were exhilarating. Ben Thanh Market offered a wide variety of goods, and bargaining for souvenirs was a fun experience. The view from the rooftop bar was stunning, and it was a great way to take in the city's skyline.

Day 9: Ho Chi Minh City
- **Morning**: Visit the War Remnants Museum to gain insight into Vietnam's recent history through powerful exhibits and photographs.
- **Afternoon**: Explore Notre-Dame Cathedral Basilica of Saigon and the Saigon Central Post Office, both fine examples of French colonial architecture.
- **Evening**: Enjoy the city's nightlife in District 1, where you can find a variety of bars, clubs, and restaurants.

Personal Experience: The War Remnants Museum was a poignant experience, providing a deep understanding of the Vietnam War from the Vietnamese perspective. Notre-Dame Cathedral and the Saigon Central Post Office were beautiful architectural landmarks, and exploring District 1's nightlife was a lively and enjoyable way to spend the evening.

Day 10: Cu Chi Tunnels and Departure
- **Morning**: Take a day trip to the Cu Chi Tunnels, an extensive network of underground tunnels used during the Vietnam War. Learn about the history and significance of the tunnels and experience crawling through a section of the tunnels.
- **Afternoon**: Return to Ho Chi Minh City and explore any sights you may have missed, or relax at a local cafe.
- **Evening**: Transfer to the airport for your departure flight.

Personal Experience: Visiting the Cu Chi Tunnels was a fascinating and educational experience. Crawling through the narrow tunnels gave me a glimpse into the challenges faced by soldiers during the war. It was a powerful way to end my trip to Vietnam, leaving me with a deep appreciation for the country's history and resilience.

14-Day Itinerary

A 14-day trip to Vietnam allows you to explore the country's diverse landscapes, rich history, and vibrant culture in depth. Here's a detailed day-by-day itinerary to help you make the most of your visit to this captivating country.

Day 1: Arrival in Hanoi

- **Morning:** Arrive in Hanoi and check into your hotel. Take some time to rest and refresh after your journey.
- **Afternoon**: Explore the Old Quarter, where you can wander through narrow streets filled with vendors, cafes, and shops. Try local delicacies like pho and banh mi.
- **Evening**: Visit Hoan Kiem Lake, take a leisurely walk around the lake, and visit Ngoc Son Temple. Enjoy a traditional water puppet show at the Thang Long Water Puppet Theatre.

Personal Experience: During my visit to Hanoi, I was captivated by the charm of the Old Quarter. Strolling through the bustling streets, I indulged in delicious street food and discovered hidden gems in the local markets. The highlight of my trip was visiting Hoan Kiem Lake and watching the traditional water puppet show, which was both entertaining and culturally enriching.

Day 2: Hanoi
- **Morning**: Tour the Ho Chi Minh Mausoleum and learn about the history of Vietnam's revolutionary leader. Visit the Presidential Palace and One Pillar Pagoda nearby.
- **Afternoon**: Discover the Temple of Literature, Vietnam's first national university, and enjoy the peaceful gardens. Visit the Vietnam Museum of Ethnology to learn about the diverse ethnic groups in Vietnam.
- **Evening**: Explore Hanoi's street food scene in the Old Quarter and sample dishes like bun cha and egg coffee.

Personal Experience: Visiting the Ho Chi Minh Mausoleum was a moving experience, and learning about the life and legacy of Ho Chi Minh provided valuable insights into Vietnam's history. The Temple of Literature was a serene escape from the city's hustle and bustle, and the Vietnam Museum of Ethnology offered a fascinating look into the country's cultural diversity.

Day 3: Hanoi to Ha Long Bay
- **Morning**: Depart from Hanoi and take a scenic drive to Ha Long Bay.
- **Afternoon**: Board a cruise and explore the stunning limestone karsts and emerald waters of Ha Long Bay. Visit caves and floating villages.
- **Evening**: Enjoy dinner on the cruise and relax under the stars.

Personal Experience: The cruise through Ha Long Bay was a highlight of my trip. The breathtaking scenery of limestone karsts rising from the emerald waters was truly mesmerizing. Visiting the caves and floating villages provided a glimpse into the local way of life, and enjoying dinner under the stars on the deck of the cruise was a magical experience.

Day 4: Ha Long Bay
- **Morning**: Continue cruising through Ha Long Bay, go kayaking, and swim in the clear waters.
- **Afternoon**: Return to the mainland and transfer back to Hanoi.
- **Evening:** Spend your last evening in Hanoi, exploring any sights you may have missed or relaxing at a local cafe.

Personal Experience: Kayaking in Ha Long Bay allowed me to explore hidden corners and get up close to the stunning rock formations. Swimming in the clear waters was refreshing, and the entire experience left me in awe of the natural beauty of the bay.

Day 5: Hanoi to Hoi An
- **Morning**: Fly from Hanoi to Da Nang and transfer to Hoi An.
- **Afternoon**: Wander through Hoi An Ancient Town, visiting historic houses, temples, and the Japanese Covered Bridge.
- **Evening**: Enjoy the vibrant atmosphere of Hoi An and dine at a riverside restaurant.

Personal Experience: Hoi An's enchanting beauty and rich history made it one of my favorite destinations in Vietnam. Wandering through the lantern-lit streets, I discovered hidden gems and indulged in delicious local cuisine. The Japanese Covered Bridge and historic houses were fascinating to explore, and dining by the riverside was a delightful experience.

Day 6: Hoi An
- **Morning:** Relax on An Bang Beach, soaking up the sun and enjoying the crystal-clear waters.
- **Afternoon**: Explore the local markets and take a traditional cooking class to learn how to make Vietnamese dishes.
- **Evening**: Experience the Hoi An Lantern Festival if your visit coincides with the event, and enjoy the magical atmosphere as the town lights up with lanterns.

Personal Experience: Relaxing on An Bang Beach was the perfect way to unwind and enjoy the natural beauty of the area. The cooking class was a highlight, as I learned how to make traditional Vietnamese dishes and gained a deeper appreciation for the country's culinary heritage. The Hoi An Lantern Festival was a magical experience, with the entire town illuminated by colorful lanterns.

Day 7: Hoi An to Da Nang
- **Morning**: Spend the morning in Hoi An, exploring any sights you may have missed.
- **Afternoon**: Transfer to Da Nang and visit the Marble Mountains, where you can explore the caves and temples and enjoy panoramic views of the city and coastline.
- **Evening**: Relax on My Khe Beach and enjoy a seafood dinner at a beachfront restaurant.

Personal Experience: The Marble Mountains were a fascinating destination, with intricate cave systems and beautiful temples to explore. The views from the top were breathtaking, and it was a great way to spend an afternoon. Relaxing on My Khe Beach and enjoying fresh seafood while watching the sunset was a perfect end to the day.

Day 8: Travel to Hue
- **Morning**: Take a scenic train ride or drive to Hue.
- **Afternoon**: Visit the Imperial City and learn about the Nguyen Dynasty. Explore the Forbidden Purple City and the surrounding gardens.

- **Evening**: Explore the local night market and try local delicacies.

Personal Experience: The train ride to Hue offered stunning views of the countryside and coastline. Visiting the Imperial City was like stepping back in time, and learning about the Nguyen Dynasty provided valuable historical context. The night market in Hue was vibrant and offered a variety of delicious street food.

Day 9: Hue
- **Morning**: Visit Thien Mu Pagoda, a beautiful riverside pagoda with historical significance. Explore the Tombs of the Emperors, including the tombs of Minh Mang and Khai Dinh.
- **Afternoon**: Take a boat ride along the Perfume River, enjoying the scenic views and stopping at traditional villages.
- **Evening**: Enjoy a traditional Hue cuisine dinner at a local restaurant.

Personal Experience: Thien Mu Pagoda was a serene and picturesque site, and the Tombs of the Emperors were architectural masterpieces. The boat ride along the Perfume River was a relaxing way to take in the natural beauty of the area, and the traditional Hue cuisine dinner was a culinary delight.

Day 10: Hue
- **Morning**: Explore any remaining sights in Hue, such as the Dong Ba Market or the Hue Royal Antiquities Museum.
- **Afternoon**: Relax at your hotel or take a cycling tour of the countryside to visit local villages and rice paddies.
- **Evening**: Transfer to the airport for a flight to Ho Chi Minh City.

Personal Experience: Exploring the local market and museum added depth to my understanding of Hue's history and culture. The cycling tour through the countryside was a refreshing and immersive experience, allowing me to connect with the local way of life.

Day 11: Travel to Ho Chi Minh City
- **Morning**: Arrive in Ho Chi Minh City and check into your hotel. Take some time to rest and refresh after your journey.
- **Afternoon**: Visit Ben Thanh Market and explore the bustling stalls, where you can shop for souvenirs and try local street food.
- **Evening**: Dine at a rooftop bar and enjoy panoramic views of the city skyline.

Personal Experience: Ho Chi Minh City's dynamic energy and vibrant markets were exhilarating. Ben Thanh Market offered a wide variety of goods, and bargaining for souvenirs was a fun experience. The view from the rooftop bar was stunning, and it was a great way to take in the city's skyline.

Day 12: Ho Chi Minh City
- **Morning**: Visit the War Remnants Museum to gain insight into Vietnam's recent history through powerful exhibits and photographs.
- **Afternoon**: Explore Notre-Dame Cathedral Basilica of Saigon and the Saigon Central Post Office, both fine

examples of French colonial architecture.
- **Evening**: Enjoy the city's nightlife in District 1, where you can find a variety of bars, clubs, and restaurants.

Personal Experience: The War Remnants Museum was a poignant experience, providing a deep understanding of the Vietnam War from the Vietnamese perspective. Notre-Dame Cathedral and the Saigon Central Post Office were beautiful architectural landmarks, and exploring District 1's nightlife was a lively and enjoyable way to spend the evening.

Day 13: Mekong Delta
- **Morning**: Take a day trip to the Mekong Delta, where you can visit floating markets, enjoy a boat ride through the canals, and explore local villages.
- **Afternoon**: Taste tropical fruits and sample local cuisine at a riverside restaurant. Visit traditional workshops to see how local products are made.
- **Evening**: Return to Ho Chi Minh City and relax at your hotel.

Personal Experience: The Mekong Delta was a fascinating and vibrant destination. The floating markets were bustling with activity, and the boat ride through the canals offered a unique perspective of the region. Tasting fresh tropical fruits and visiting traditional workshops added to the immersive experience.

Day 14: Cu Chi Tunnels and Departure
- **Morning**: Take a day trip to the Cu Chi Tunnels, an extensive network of underground tunnels used during the Vietnam War. Learn about the history and significance of the tunnels and experience crawling through a section of the tunnels.
- **Afternoon**: Return to Ho Chi Minh City and explore any sights you may have missed, or relax at a local cafe.
- **Evening**: Transfer to the airport for your departure flight.

Personal Experience: Visiting the Cu Chi Tunnels was a fascinating and educational experience. Crawling through the narrow tunnels gave me a glimpse into the challenges faced by soldiers during the war. It was a powerful way to end my trip to Vietnam, leaving me with a deep appreciation for the country's history and resilience.

Special Interest Itineraries

Vietnam is a land of diverse experiences, and whether you're interested in culture, adventure, or beach holidays, there's something for everyone. Here are some detailed itineraries for special interests, including highlights and what to expect.

Cultural Itinerary
Day 1: Arrival in Hanoi
- **Morning**: Arrive in Hanoi and check into your hotel. Rest and refresh after your journey.
- **Afternoon**: Explore the Old Quarter, where you can wander through narrow streets filled with vendors, cafes, and shops. Try local delicacies like pho and banh mi.
- **Evening**: Visit Hoan Kiem Lake, take a leisurely walk around the lake, and visit Ngoc Son Temple. Enjoy a

traditional water puppet show at the Thang Long Water Puppet Theatre.

What to Expect: A vibrant introduction to Hanoi's culture and cuisine, with a mix of historic sites and local experiences.

Day 2: Hanoi
- **Morning**: Tour the Ho Chi Minh Mausoleum and learn about the history of Vietnam's revolutionary leader. Visit the Presidential Palace and One Pillar Pagoda nearby.
- **Afternoon**: Discover the Temple of Literature, Vietnam's first national university, and enjoy the peaceful gardens. Visit the Vietnam Museum of Ethnology to learn about the diverse ethnic groups in Vietnam.
- **Evening**: Explore Hanoi's street food scene in the Old Quarter and sample dishes like bun cha and egg coffee.

What to Expect: A deep dive into Hanoi's historical and cultural landmarks, along with a taste of local cuisine.

Day 3: Travel to Hue
- **Morning**: Take a scenic train ride or flight to Hue.
- **Afternoon**: Visit the Imperial City and learn about the Nguyen Dynasty. Explore the Forbidden Purple City and the surrounding gardens.
- **Evening**: Explore the local night market and try local delicacies.

What to Expect: A journey through Vietnam's imperial history, with visits to palaces, temples, and bustling markets.

Day 4: Hue
- **Morning**: Visit Thien Mu Pagoda, a beautiful riverside pagoda with historical significance. Explore the Tombs of the Emperors, including the tombs of Minh Mang and Khai Dinh.
- **Afternoon**: Take a boat ride along the Perfume River, enjoying the scenic views and stopping at traditional villages.
- **Evening**: Enjoy a traditional Hue cuisine dinner at a local restaurant.

What to Expect: A day filled with historical and spiritual sites, along with a relaxing boat ride and local cuisine.

Day 5: Travel to Hoi An
- **Morning:** Drive or take a bus to Hoi An.
- **Afternoon**: Wander through the ancient town and visit the Japanese Covered Bridge. Explore the historic houses and temples.
- **Evening**: Take a traditional cooking class and learn how to make Vietnamese dishes.

What to Expect: A blend of cultural exploration and hands-on experiences in a charming ancient town.

Day 6: Hoi An
- **Morning**: Relax on An Bang Beach, soaking up the sun and enjoying the crystal-clear waters.
- **Afternoon**: Explore the local markets and participate in a lantern-making workshop.

- **Evening**: Experience the Hoi An Lantern Festival if your visit coincides with the event.

What to Expect: A day of relaxation, creativity, and magical evening celebrations.

Day 7: Departure from Hoi An
- **Morning**: Spend your last morning in Hoi An, exploring any sights you may have missed or doing some last-minute shopping.
- **Afternoon**: Transfer to Da Nang Airport for your departure flight.

Highlights: Old Quarter (Hanoi), Hoan Kiem Lake, Ho Chi Minh Mausoleum, Temple of Literature, Vietnam Museum of Ethnology, Imperial City (Hue), Thien Mu Pagoda, Tombs of the Emperors, Perfume River, Hoi An Ancient Town, Japanese Covered Bridge, An Bang Beach, Hoi An Lantern Festival.

Adventure Itinerary

Day 1: Arrival in Sapa
- **Morning**: Arrive in Sapa and check into your hotel. Rest and refresh after your journey.
- **Afternoon**: Trek through the terraced rice fields and visit local ethnic minority villages.
- **Evening**: Enjoy a traditional dinner and cultural performance at your hotel.

What to Expect: A scenic introduction to Sapa's stunning landscapes and vibrant local culture.

Day 2: Sapa
- **Morning**: Continue trekking through the rice fields and explore more villages.
- **Afternoon**: Climb Mount Fansipan, the highest peak in Indochina, or take the cable car for breathtaking views.
- **Evening**: Relax at your hotel and enjoy the serene mountain atmosphere.

What to Expect: An adventurous day of trekking and stunning panoramic views.

Day 3: Travel to Ha Long Bay
- **Morning**: Depart from Sapa and take a scenic drive to Ha Long Bay.
- **Afternoon**: Board a cruise and explore the stunning limestone karsts and emerald waters of Ha Long Bay. Visit caves and floating villages.
- **Evening**: Enjoy dinner on the cruise and relax under the stars.

What to Expect: A picturesque journey from the mountains to the sea, with a relaxing cruise experience.

Day 4: Ha Long Bay
- **Morning**: Continue cruising through Ha Long Bay, go kayaking, and swim in the clear waters.
- **Afternoon:** Return to the mainland and transfer to Hanoi.
- **Evening**: Spend your last evening in Hanoi, exploring any sights you may have missed.

What to Expect: A day of water-based activities and stunning natural beauty.

Day 5: Travel to Phong Nha-Ke Bang National Park
- **Morning**: Fly from Hanoi to Dong Hoi and transfer to Phong Nha-Ke Bang National Park.
- **Afternoon**: Explore the stunning caves, including Paradise Cave and Phong Nha Cave.
- **Evening**: Enjoy dinner at a local restaurant and relax at your hotel.

What to Expect: An awe-inspiring exploration of some of the world's most impressive caves.

Day 6: Phong Nha-Ke Bang National Park
- **Morning**: Take a boat trip along the Son River to visit the Dark Cave. Enjoy activities like zip-lining and swimming in the underground river.
- **Afternoon**: Continue exploring the park's other attractions, such as the Botanical Garden and the Mooc Spring Eco-Trail.
- **Evening**: Return to your hotel and relax.

What to Expect: A day of adventure and exploration in one of Vietnam's natural wonders.

Day 7: Travel to Da Nang and Hoi An
- **Morning**: Fly from Dong Hoi to Da Nang and transfer to Hoi An.
- **Afternoon**: Wander through Hoi An Ancient Town and visit the Japanese Covered Bridge.
- **Evening**: Dine at a riverside restaurant and enjoy the vibrant atmosphere.

What to Expect: A transition from adventure to cultural exploration in a charming town.

Day 8: Hoi An
- **Morning**: Go cycling through the countryside to explore local villages and rice paddies.
- **Afternoon**: Take a traditional cooking class and learn how to make Vietnamese dishes.
- **Evening**: Experience the Hoi An Lantern Festival if your visit coincides with the event.

What to Expect: A mix of outdoor activities and hands-on cultural experiences.

Day 9: Travel to Da Nang
- **Morning**: Visit the Marble Mountains and explore the caves and temples.
- **Afternoon**: Relax on My Khe Beach and enjoy water activities like surfing and paddleboarding.
- **Evening**: Walk across the Dragon Bridge and catch the fire-breathing show.

What to Expect: A day of exploration and relaxation by the beach.

Day 10: Departure from Da Nang
- **Morning**: Spend your last morning in Da Nang, exploring any sights you may have missed.
- **Afternoon**: Transfer to the airport for your departure flight.

Highlights: Terraced rice fields (Sapa), Mount Fansipan, Ha Long Bay, Paradise Cave, Phong Nha Cave, Dark Cave, Hoi An Ancient Town,

Japanese Covered Bridge, Marble Mountains, My Khe Beach, Dragon Bridge.

Beach Holidays Itinerary

Day 1: Arrival in Phu Quoc Island
- **Morning**: Arrive in Phu Quoc and check into your resort. Rest and refresh after your journey.
- **Afternoon**: Relax on Long Beach, soaking up the sun and enjoying the crystal-clear waters.
- **Evening**: Enjoy a seafood dinner at a beachfront restaurant.

What to Expect: A relaxing start to your beach holiday with sun, sea, and delicious food.

Day 2: Phu Quoc Island
- **Morning**: Visit Vinpearl Safari, Vietnam's largest wildlife conservation park.
- **Afternoon**: Explore Phu Quoc National Park and take a hike to see the diverse flora and fauna.
- **Evening**: Visit the Dinh Cau Night Market and try local street food.

What to Expect: A mix of wildlife exploration and local culture.

Day 3: Phu Quoc Island
- **Morning**: Go snorkeling or diving at the An Thoi Archipelago, known for its vibrant coral reefs and marine life.
- **Afternoon**: Relax on Bai Sao Beach, one of the most beautiful beaches on the island.
- **Evening**: Enjoy a sunset cruise around the island.

What to Expect: A day of underwater adventure and beach relaxation.

Day 4: Travel to Nha Trang
- **Morning**: Fly from Phu Quoc to Nha Trang and check into your hotel.
- **Afternoon**: Relax on Nha Trang Beach and enjoy water activities like jet skiing and parasailing.
- **Evening**: Dine at a beachfront restaurant and enjoy fresh seafood.

What to Expect: A day of travel followed by beach relaxation and thrilling water sports.

Day 5: Nha Trang
- **Morning:** Visit Vinpearl Land, an amusement park with rides, water slides, and an aquarium.
- **Afternoon**: Explore the Po Nagar Cham Towers, ancient Hindu temples with stunning views of the city and coast.
- **Evening**: Take a sunset cruise along the Nha Trang coastline.

What to Expect: A mix of fun and cultural exploration, with stunning sunset views.

Day 6: Nha Trang
- **Morning**: Go snorkeling or diving at Hon Mun Marine Protected Area, known for its coral reefs and marine life.
- **Afternoon**: Relax at Thap Ba Hot Springs and enjoy a mud bath and spa treatments.
- **Evening**: Enjoy a beachside barbecue at your hotel or a local restaurant.

What to Expect: A day of underwater exploration and relaxing spa experiences.

Day 7: Travel to Da Nang and Hoi An
- **Morning**: Fly from Nha Trang to Da Nang and transfer to Hoi An.
- **Afternoon**: Wander through Hoi An Ancient Town, visiting historic houses, temples, and the Japanese Covered Bridge.
- **Evening**: Dine at a riverside restaurant and enjoy the vibrant atmosphere.

What to Expect: A transition from beach relaxation to cultural exploration in a charming town.

Day 8: Hoi An
- **Morning**: Go cycling through the countryside to explore local villages and rice paddies.
- **Afternoon**: Relax on An Bang Beach and soak up the sun.
- **Evening**: Experience the Hoi An Lantern Festival if your visit coincides with the event.

What to Expect: A mix of outdoor activities and beach relaxation, with magical evening celebrations.

Day 9: Travel to Da Nang
- **Morning**: Visit the Marble Mountains and explore the caves and temples.
- **Afternoon**: Relax on My Khe Beach and enjoy water activities like surfing and paddleboarding.
- **Evening**: Walk across the Dragon Bridge and catch the fire-breathing show.

What to Expect: A day of exploration and relaxation by the beach.

Day 10: Departure from Da Nang
- **Morning**: Spend your last morning in Da Nang, exploring any sights you may have missed.
- **Afternoon**: Transfer to the airport for your departure flight.

Chapter 3: Accommodations

Hotels and Resorts

When it comes to accommodations in Vietnam, hotels and resorts offer a wide range of options to suit every traveler's needs and preferences. From luxurious five-star resorts with world-class amenities to budget-friendly hotels that provide comfort and convenience, you'll find something that matches your style and budget.

Hotels and resorts in Vietnam are known for their excellent service, modern facilities, and prime locations. Whether you're exploring the bustling cities, relaxing on beautiful beaches, or discovering the serene countryside, these accommodations provide a comfortable and enjoyable base for your adventures. In major cities like Hanoi and Ho Chi Minh City, you'll find a mix of international hotel chains and boutique hotels that combine modern comforts with traditional Vietnamese design. Coastal cities like Da Nang and Nha Trang boast resorts with stunning ocean views and easy access to the beach, making them ideal for a relaxing getaway.

Luxury Hotels and Resorts

Description: Luxury hotels and resorts in Vietnam offer world-class amenities, exceptional service, and stunning locations. These establishments provide an unparalleled experience, combining modern comforts with

Vietnamese hospitality and charm. From beachfront resorts to city-center luxury hotels, these accommodations cater to travelers seeking the finest in comfort, style, and convenience.

Examples of Luxury Hotels and Resorts:
1. **The Reverie Saigon (Ho Chi Minh City):**
   - Located in the heart of District 1, this opulent hotel offers lavish rooms, exquisite dining options, and breathtaking views of the city skyline.

2. **InterContinental Danang Sun Peninsula Resort (Da Nang):**
   - Nestled in the Son Tra Peninsula, this resort features stunning ocean views, a private beach, and award-winning restaurants.

3. **Sofitel Legend Metropole Hanoi (Hanoi):**
   - A historic luxury hotel in the French Quarter, known for its elegant colonial architecture, luxurious rooms, and fine dining.

4. **JW Marriott Phu Quoc Emerald Bay Resort & Spa (Phu Quoc Island):**
   - A beachfront resort designed by Bill Bensley, offering unique architecture, luxurious accommodations, and a range of activities.

5. **Six Senses Ninh Van Bay (Nha Trang):**
   - An eco-luxury resort located on a secluded bay, offering private villas, a world-class spa, and stunning natural surroundings.

Highlights:

- **Exceptional Service**: Luxury hotels and resorts pride themselves on providing top-notch service, with attentive staff ready to cater to your every need.
- **Prime Locations**: Whether situated in bustling city centers or serene beachfront locations, these accommodations offer easy access to key attractions and beautiful views.
- **World-Class Amenities**: Guests can enjoy a range of amenities, including infinity pools, private beaches, spas, gourmet restaurants, and fitness centers.
- **Elegant Design**: These properties often feature stylish and sophisticated decor, blending modern design with local cultural elements.

Amenities:
- **Swimming Pools and Spas:** Many luxury resorts offer multiple pools, including infinity pools, as well as extensive spa facilities with a variety of treatments.
- **Fine Dining**: On-site restaurants serve gourmet cuisine, often with a focus on local flavors and international dishes.
- **Fitness Centers**: State-of-the-art gyms and fitness facilities are available for guests to stay active during their stay.
- **Concierge Services**: Personalized assistance with tour bookings, transportation, and special requests.
- **Exclusive Activities**: Some resorts offer unique experiences such as private yacht cruises, cooking classes, and guided tours.

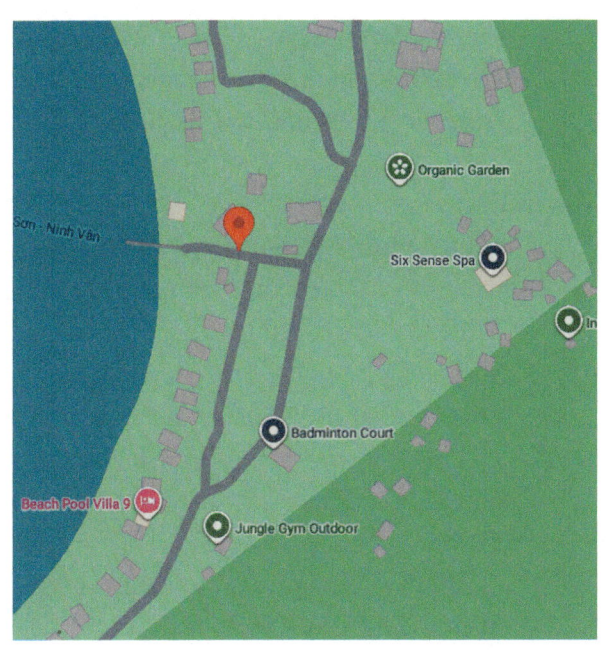

Pricing:
- **The Reverie Saigon:** Prices generally range from $300 to $800+ per night.
- **InterContinental Danang Sun Peninsula Resort:** Prices typically range from $400 to $1,200+ per night.
- **Sofitel Legend Metropole Hanoi:** Prices usually range from $250 to $700+ per night.
- **JW Marriott Phu Quoc Emerald Bay Resort & Spa:** Prices generally range from $350 to $900+ per night.
- **Six Senses Ninh Van Bay:** Prices typically range from $500 to $1,500+ per night.

What to Expect:
- **High Standards of Comfort**: Luxurious and spacious rooms with premium bedding, high-quality furnishings, and modern amenities.
- **Impeccable Service:** Friendly and professional staff providing personalized and attentive service.
- **Elegant Ambiance**: Stylish interiors, beautifully landscaped grounds, and a tranquil atmosphere.
- **Exclusive Experiences**: Opportunities to indulge in unique activities and experiences tailored to your preferences.

Staying at The Reverie Saigon was an unforgettable experience. The opulent decor and impeccable service made me feel like royalty. The panoramic views of Ho Chi Minh City from my room were breathtaking, and the gourmet dining options exceeded my expectations. At the InterContinental Danang Sun Peninsula Resort, I was captivated by the stunning ocean views and the resort's beautiful design. The private beach and luxurious spa treatments provided the perfect setting for relaxation. My stay at Sofitel Legend Metropole Hanoi was equally memorable, with its elegant colonial architecture and historical charm. The hotel's prime location in the French Quarter made it easy to explore Hanoi's cultural and historical sites.

Mid-Range Hotels

Description: Mid-range hotels in Vietnam offer comfortable stays with a good balance of quality and affordability. These hotels provide essential amenities and services to ensure a pleasant experience without the high price tag of luxury accommodations. They are often well-located, making it easy for travelers to explore nearby attractions and enjoy the local culture.

Examples of Mid-Range Hotels:
1. **Hanoi La Siesta Hotel & Spa (Hanoi):**

- Located in the Old Quarter, this hotel offers comfortable rooms, a spa, and a rooftop bar with city views.

2. **Liberty Central Saigon Riverside Hotel (Ho Chi Minh City)**:
   - Situated along the Saigon River, this hotel features modern rooms, a rooftop pool, and convenient access to popular landmarks.

3. **Vanda Hotel (Da Nang)**:
   - Centrally located near the Dragon Bridge, this hotel offers contemporary rooms, a spa, and a rooftop bar with panoramic views of the city.

4. **Almanity Hoi An Wellness Resort (Hoi An)**:
   - A wellness-focused resort offering comfortable accommodations, a spa, and daily wellness activities.

5. **Sunrise Nha Trang Beach Hotel & Spa (Nha Trang)**:
   - A beachfront hotel with modern amenities, multiple dining options, and a relaxing spa.

Highlights:
- **Affordable Comfort**: Mid-range hotels provide a comfortable stay with essential amenities at a reasonable price.
- **Convenient Locations**: Many mid-range hotels are located in central areas, making it easy to explore nearby attractions.
- **Good Amenities**: Guests can enjoy amenities such as WiFi, on-site dining, fitness centers, and spa services.

Amenities:
- **Comfortable Rooms**: Well-furnished rooms with modern amenities like WiFi, air conditioning, and flat-screen TVs.
- **On-Site Dining**: Restaurants and cafes serving a variety of local and international dishes.
- **Fitness Centers**: Gyms and fitness facilities for guests to stay active during their stay.
- **Spa Services:** Some hotels offer spa treatments and wellness activities.
- **Concierge Services**: Assistance with tour bookings, transportation, and local recommendations.

Pricing:
- **Hanoi La Siesta Hotel & Spa:** Prices generally range from $70 to $150 per night.
- **Liberty Central Saigon Riverside Hotel**: Prices typically range from $80 to $160 per night.
- **Vanda Hotel**: Prices usually range from $60 to $130 per night.
- **Almanity Hoi An Wellness Resort:** Prices generally range from $90 to $180 per night.
- **Sunrise Nha Trang Beach Hotel & Spa**: Prices typically range from $100 to $200 per night.

What to Expect:
- **Quality and Comfort**: Mid-range hotels offer clean, comfortable, and

well-maintained rooms with modern amenities.
- **Friendly Service**: Professional and welcoming staff ready to assist with your needs.
- **Convenient Facilities**: Access to on-site dining, fitness centers, and other essential amenities.
- **Good Value**: A balance of affordability and quality, providing a pleasant stay without breaking the bank.

Staying at Hanoi La Siesta Hotel & Spa was a delightful experience. The hotel's central location in the Old Quarter made it easy to explore Hanoi's bustling streets and historic sites. The rooms were comfortable, and the rooftop bar offered stunning views of the city. At Liberty Central Saigon Riverside Hotel, I enjoyed the modern amenities and convenient access to popular landmarks along the Saigon River. The rooftop pool was a great place to relax after a day of sightseeing. In Da Nang, Vanda Hotel provided a comfortable stay with beautiful views of the Dragon Bridge. The hotel's spa services were a perfect way to unwind after exploring the city. Almanity Hoi An Wellness Resort offered a unique wellness-focused experience, with daily activities and a relaxing spa that made my stay in Hoi An truly rejuvenating.

Boutique Hotels

Description: Boutique hotels in Vietnam offer a unique and charming experience, characterized by personalized service, distinctive design, and attention to detail. These hotels are often smaller in size, allowing for a more intimate and cozy atmosphere. Boutique hotels combine modern comforts with local cultural elements, providing a memorable and authentic stay for travelers seeking something special.

Examples of Boutique Hotels:

1. **La Siesta Premium Hang Be (Hanoi):**
   - Located in the heart of the Old Quarter, this hotel features elegant decor, cozy rooms, and a rooftop bar with panoramic views.

2. **Villa Song Saigon (Ho Chi Minh City):**
   - A riverside boutique hotel offering luxurious rooms, a tranquil garden, and a relaxing pool area.

3. **Fusion Suites Danang Beach (Da Nang):**
   - A modern boutique hotel with stylish suites, a rooftop pool, and a focus on wellness and relaxation.

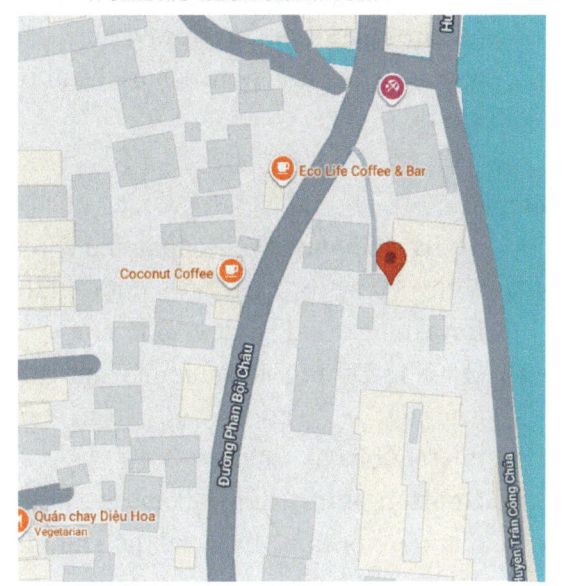

4. **Little Riverside Hoi An - A Luxury Hotel & Spa (Hoi An):**
   - Situated along the Thu Bon River, this boutique hotel offers beautifully designed rooms, a riverside pool, and a relaxing spa.

5. **Mia Resort Nha Trang (Nha Trang):**
   - An eco-friendly boutique resort with private villas, stunning ocean views, and a focus on sustainability and relaxation.

Highlights:
- **Personalized Service:** Boutique hotels pride themselves on offering attentive and personalized service to make guests feel at home.
- **Unique Design**: Each boutique hotel has its own distinct character, often incorporating local art, culture, and history into its design.
- **Intimate Atmosphere**: Smaller size and fewer rooms create a cozy and intimate environment.
- **Prime Locations**: Many boutique hotels are situated in central or picturesque locations, providing easy access to attractions and beautiful views.

Amenities:
- **Stylish Rooms**: Well-appointed rooms with unique decor, comfortable furnishings, and modern amenities.
- **On-Site Dining**: Restaurants and cafes offering a variety of local and international cuisine.
- **Rooftop Bars:** Some boutique hotels feature rooftop bars with stunning views of the city or surroundings.
- **Spa Services**: Many boutique hotels offer spa treatments and wellness services.
- **Personalized Assistance:** Concierge services to help with tour bookings, transportation, and local recommendations.

Pricing:
- **La Siesta Premium Hang Be**: Prices generally range from $90 to $180 per night.
- **Villa Song Saigon**: Prices typically range from $120 to $250 per night.
- **Fusion Suites Danang Beach**: Prices usually range from $100 to $200 per night.
- **Little Riverside Hoi An:** Prices generally range from $80 to $160 per night.
- **Mia Resort Nha Trang:** Prices typically range from $150 to $300 per night.

What to Expect:
- **Charming and Unique Design**: Each boutique hotel offers a distinct ambiance with stylish decor and personalized touches.
- **High-Quality Comfort**: Comfortable rooms with modern amenities, ensuring a pleasant stay.
- **Attentive Service**: Friendly and attentive staff providing personalized assistance.
- **Intimate and Cozy Environment:** A smaller, more intimate setting that allows for a relaxing and enjoyable experience.

Staying at La Siesta Premium Hang Be in Hanoi was a delightful experience. The hotel's central location in the Old Quarter made it easy to explore the city's vibrant streets and historic sites. The rooftop bar offered stunning views of Hanoi, and the personalized service made me feel truly welcome. At Villa Song Saigon, the tranquil riverside setting provided a peaceful retreat from the bustling city. The luxurious rooms and beautiful garden made it a perfect place to relax. Fusion Suites Danang Beach offered a modern and stylish experience with a focus on wellness. The rooftop pool and spa treatments were highlights of my stay. Little Riverside Hoi An provided a charming riverside experience with beautifully designed rooms and a relaxing pool area. Mia Resort Nha Trang's eco-friendly approach and stunning ocean views made it a memorable and sustainable getaway.

Budget Hotels

Description: Budget hotels in Vietnam provide affordable and comfortable accommodations for travelers looking to save money without sacrificing quality. These hotels offer essential amenities and services, ensuring a pleasant stay for budget-conscious travelers. Budget hotels are often well-located, making it easy to explore nearby attractions and enjoy the local culture.

Examples of Budget Hotels:
1. **Hanoi Graceful Hotel (Hanoi):**
   - Located in the Old Quarter, this hotel offers clean and comfortable rooms with modern amenities at an affordable price.

2. **My Hotel & Spa (Ho Chi Minh City):**
   - A budget-friendly hotel in District 1, providing cozy rooms, a spa, and convenient access to popular landmarks.

3. **Gold Summer Hotel (Da Nang):**
   - Situated near My Khe Beach, this hotel offers budget accommodations with essential amenities and easy beach access.

4. **Hoi An Dream City Hotel (Hoi An):**
   - A budget hotel located close to the Ancient Town, offering simple yet comfortable rooms and friendly service.

5. **Nha Trang Beach Hotel (Nha Trang):**
   - A budget hotel located near the beach, providing basic accommodations and convenient access to the city's attractions.

Highlights:
- **Affordability:** Budget hotels offer an economical option for travelers, allowing them to save money while still enjoying a comfortable stay.
- **Convenient Locations:** Many budget hotels are centrally located, providing easy access to attractions, dining, and transportation.
- **Essential Amenities:** Budget hotels provide essential amenities, such as free WiFi, air conditioning, and clean, comfortable rooms.

Amenities:
- **Comfortable Rooms:** Basic but well-maintained rooms with essential amenities like WiFi, air conditioning, and flat-screen TVs.
- **On-Site Dining**: Some budget hotels have on-site restaurants or cafes offering simple meals and beverages.

- **Laundry Services**: On-site laundry services or self-service laundry facilities.
- **Concierge Services**: Assistance with tour bookings, transportation, and local recommendations.
- **Free WiFi**: Complimentary internet access in rooms and public areas.

Pricing:
- **Hanoi Graceful Hotel:** Prices generally range from $20 to $40 per night.
- **My Hotel & Spa:** Prices typically range from $25 to $50 per night.
- **Gold Summer Hotel:** Prices usually range from $15 to $35 per night.
- **Hoi An Dream City Hotel:** Prices generally range from $20 to $40 per night.
- **Nha Trang Beach Hotel:** Prices typically range from $20 to $40 per night.

What to Expect:
- **Basic Comfort**: Clean and comfortable rooms with essential amenities, ensuring a pleasant stay without luxury frills.
- **Friendly Service**: Welcoming and helpful staff ready to assist with your needs.
- **Good Value**: Affordable pricing that allows you to save money while still enjoying a comfortable stay.
- **Convenient Facilities**: Access to basic amenities such as WiFi, on-site dining, and laundry services.

Staying at Hanoi Graceful Hotel provided a comfortable and budget-friendly experience. The hotel's central location in the Old Quarter made it easy to explore Hanoi's vibrant streets and historic sites. The rooms were clean and well-maintained, and the staff were friendly and helpful. At My Hotel & Spa in Ho Chi Minh City, I enjoyed the cozy rooms and convenient access to popular landmarks in District 1. The on-site spa was a nice bonus for relaxation after a day of sightseeing. In Da Nang, Gold Summer Hotel offered budget accommodations near My Khe Beach, allowing me to enjoy the beach without breaking the bank. Hoi An Dream City Hotel provided a simple yet comfortable stay close to the Ancient Town, with friendly service and easy access to the town's attractions. Nha Trang Beach Hotel's proximity to the beach and affordable pricing made it a great choice for budget-conscious travelers looking to explore the city's coastal attractions.

Guesthouses and Hostels

Guesthouses

Description: Guesthouses in Vietnam are family-run establishments that provide a homely and welcoming environment. They offer comfortable and affordable accommodations with essential amenities. Guesthouses are often located in central areas, making it easy for travelers to explore nearby attractions and immerse themselves in the local culture.

Examples of Guesthouses:

1. **Hanoi Guesthouse (Hanoi):**
   - A cozy guesthouse located in the Old Quarter, offering clean rooms, friendly service, and a central location.

2. **Ngoc Thao Guesthouse (Ho Chi Minh City):**
   - A budget-friendly guesthouse in District 1, providing comfortable rooms and a welcoming atmosphere.

3. **Ha An Hotel (Hoi An):**
   - A charming guesthouse near the Ancient Town, offering beautifully decorated rooms and a peaceful garden.

4. **Hue Serene Palace Hotel (Hue):**
   - A well-rated guesthouse with modern amenities, friendly staff, and convenient access to the city's attractions.

5. **Sapa Elite Hotel (Sapa):**
   - A cozy guesthouse with stunning views of the mountains and comfortable rooms, perfect for exploring Sapa.

Highlights:

- **Homely Atmosphere**: Guesthouses provide a warm and welcoming environment, often run by local families who offer personalized service.
- **Affordable Comfort**: Comfortable accommodations at budget-friendly prices.
- **Cultural Immersion**: Opportunities to interact with local hosts and learn about Vietnamese culture.

Amenities:

- **Comfortable Rooms**: Clean and well-maintained rooms with essential amenities like WiFi, air conditioning, and private bathrooms.
- **On-Site Dining**: Some guesthouses have on-site restaurants or offer home-cooked meals.
- **Laundry Services:** On-site laundry services or self-service laundry facilities.
- **Concierge Services**: Assistance with tour bookings, transportation, and local recommendations.
- **Free WiFi:** Complimentary internet access in rooms and public areas.

Pricing:

- **Hanoi Guesthouse:** Prices generally range from $20 to $40 per night.
- **Ngoc Thao Guesthouse:** Prices typically range from $15 to $30 per night.
- **Ha An Hotel:** Prices usually range from $25 to $50 per night.
- **Hue Serene Palace Hotel**: Prices generally range from $20 to $40 per night.

- **Sapa Elite Hotel:** Prices typically range from $30 to $60 per night.

What to Expect:
- **Warm and Welcoming Service:** Friendly and helpful hosts ready to assist with your needs.
- **Clean and Comfortable Rooms**: Basic but well-maintained accommodations with essential amenities.
- **Cultural Insights**: Opportunities to learn about the local culture and interact with your hosts.
- **Affordable Pricing**: Budget-friendly rates that provide good value for money.

Staying at Hanoi Guesthouse provided a cozy and budget-friendly experience. The central location in the Old Quarter made it easy to explore Hanoi's vibrant streets and historic sites. The hosts were friendly and offered great recommendations for local attractions. At Ha An Hotel in Hoi An, I enjoyed the beautifully decorated rooms and peaceful garden. The personalized service and charming atmosphere made it a memorable stay. In Sapa, Sapa Elite Hotel offered stunning views of the mountains and comfortable rooms, making it a perfect base for exploring the region.

Hostels

Description: Hostels in Vietnam are known for their social atmosphere and budget-friendly accommodations. They often feature dormitory-style rooms with shared facilities, allowing travelers to save money and meet people from all over the world. Many hostels also offer private rooms for those who prefer more privacy. Hostels are a great choice for solo travelers and those looking to make new friends during their journey.

Examples of Hostels:

1. **Hanoi Backpackers Hostel (Hanoi):**
   - A lively hostel located in the Old Quarter, offering dormitory and private rooms, a bar, and organized social events.

2. **The Common Room Project (Ho Chi Minh City):**
   - A stylish hostel in District 5, featuring dormitory and private rooms, a rooftop terrace, and a communal kitchen.

3. **Memory Hostel (Da Nang):**
   - A modern hostel with dormitory and private rooms, a rooftop bar, and a central location near the Dragon Bridge.

4. **Vietnam Backpacker Hostels - Hoi An (Hoi An):**
   - A popular hostel offering dormitory and private rooms, a swimming pool, and organized activities for guests.

5. **Sapa Unique Hotel (Sapa):**
   - A cozy hostel with dormitory and private rooms, stunning mountain views, and a welcoming atmosphere.

Highlights:
- **Social Atmosphere**: Hostels are great for meeting fellow travelers and joining organized social events.

- **Budget-Friendly**: Affordable accommodations that help travelers save money.
- **Convenient Locations**: Many hostels are centrally located, providing easy access to attractions and transportation.

Amenities:
- **Dormitory and Private Rooms**: A mix of dormitory-style rooms and private rooms to suit different preferences.
- **Communal Areas**: Common rooms or lounges where guests can relax and socialize.
- **Rooftop Bars:** Some hostels feature rooftop bars with stunning views.
- **Free WiFi**: Complimentary internet access in rooms and public areas.
- **Laundry Facilities**: On-site laundry services or self-service laundry facilities.
- **Tours and Activities**: Organized tours, pub crawls, and other social events for guests.

Pricing:
- **Hanoi Backpackers Hostel**: Prices for dormitory beds generally range from $5 to $15 per night, and private rooms range from $20 to $40 per night.
- **The Common Room Project**: Prices for dormitory beds typically range from $10 to $20 per night, and private rooms range from $30 to $60 per night.
- **Memory Hostel**: Prices for dormitory beds usually range from $7 to $15 per night, and private rooms range from $25 to $50 per night.
- **Vietnam Backpacker Hostels - Hoi An:** Prices for dormitory beds generally range from $5 to $15 per night, and private rooms range from $20 to $40 per night.
- **Sapa Unique Hotel:** Prices for dormitory beds typically range from $10 to $20 per night, and private rooms range from $30 to $60 per night.

What to Expect:
- **Lively and Social Environment**: Opportunities to meet fellow travelers and join social events.
- **Basic Comfort**: Clean and well-maintained rooms with essential amenities.
- **Friendly Service**: Welcoming and helpful staff ready to assist with your needs.
- **Affordable Rates**: Budget-friendly pricing that provides good value for money.

Staying at Hanoi Backpackers Hostel was a fun and social experience. The lively atmosphere and organized events made it easy to meet fellow travelers. The dormitory rooms were clean and comfortable, and the rooftop bar offered great views of the city. At The Common Room Project in Ho Chi Minh City, I enjoyed the stylish decor and communal spaces. The rooftop terrace was a perfect spot to relax and socialize. Memory Hostel in Da Nang provided a modern and comfortable stay with a rooftop bar that offered stunning views of the Dragon Bridge. Vietnam Backpacker Hostels - Hoi An was a popular choice for its social activities and swimming pool, making it a great place to meet other travelers. Sapa

Unique Hotel's cozy atmosphere and stunning mountain views made it a perfect base for exploring Sapa.

Homestays

Description: Homestays in Vietnam offer a unique opportunity to immerse yourself in the local culture by staying with a Vietnamese family. These accommodations provide a warm and welcoming environment, allowing travelers to experience daily life, traditions, and customs firsthand. Homestays are often located in rural areas, offering beautiful natural surroundings and authentic experiences.

Examples of Homestays:
1. **Sapa Homestay Ta Van Village (Sapa):**
   - A traditional homestay in a Hmong village, offering a chance to experience rural life and stunning views of the terraced rice fields.

2. **Mekong Delta Homestay (Mekong Delta):**
   - A rustic homestay in the heart of the Mekong Delta, where guests can enjoy boat tours, local cuisine, and cultural activities.

3. **Hoi An Ancient House Village Resort & Spa (Hoi An):**
   - A charming homestay offering beautifully designed rooms, a peaceful garden, and traditional Vietnamese hospitality.

4. **Ha Giang Homestay (Ha Giang):**
   - A homestay in the mountainous region of Ha Giang, providing opportunities for trekking, cultural exchange, and breathtaking landscapes.

5. **Mai Chau Ecolodge (Mai Chau):**
   - An eco-friendly homestay in Mai Chau, offering comfortable accommodations, local activities, and scenic views of the rice paddies.

Highlights:
- **Cultural Immersion:** Homestays provide an authentic cultural experience, allowing travelers to learn about local customs, traditions, and daily life.
- **Personalized Service:** Staying with a local family means personalized attention and hospitality.
- **Beautiful Surroundings:** Many homestays are located in rural areas, offering stunning natural landscapes and a peaceful atmosphere.
- **Hands-On Activities:** Guests can participate in activities such as farming, cooking, and handicraft making.

Amenities:
- **Comfortable Rooms:** Basic but well-maintained rooms with essential amenities like WiFi, mosquito nets, and clean bedding.

- **Home-Cooked Meals:** Enjoy delicious meals prepared by your host family, often featuring local ingredients and traditional recipes.
- **Guided Activities:** Participate in guided activities such as trekking, boat tours, and cultural workshops.
- **Local Insights**: Hosts can provide valuable information about the area and recommend hidden gems.
- **Cultural Workshops:** Some homestays offer workshops on traditional crafts, music, and dance.

Pricing:
- **Sapa Homestay Ta Van Village:** Prices generally range from $15 to $30 per night.
- **Mekong Delta Homestay:** Prices typically range from $20 to $40 per night.
- **Hoi An Ancient House Village Resort & Spa:** Prices usually range from $30 to $70 per night.
- **Ha Giang Homestay**: Prices generally range from $15 to $30 per night.
- **Mai Chau Ecolodge:** Prices typically range from $40 to $80 per night.

What to Expect:
- **Warm and Welcoming Environment**: A friendly and hospitable atmosphere provided by your host family.
- **Immersive Cultural Experience:** Opportunities to learn about local customs, participate in daily activities, and enjoy traditional meals.
- **Basic Comfort**: Simple yet comfortable accommodations with essential amenities.
- **Beautiful Natural Surroundings:** Many homestays are situated in scenic rural areas, offering stunning views and a peaceful atmosphere.

Staying at a homestay in Sapa was a highlight of my trip. The host family was incredibly warm and welcoming, and I enjoyed participating in their daily activities, such as helping with farming and learning to cook traditional dishes. The stunning views of the terraced rice fields and the opportunity to learn about the local culture made it an unforgettable experience. In the Mekong Delta, I stayed at a rustic homestay where I joined a boat tour of the floating markets and tasted fresh tropical fruits. The authentic experiences and the chance to connect with local people made my stay truly special. At Mai Chau Ecolodge, I appreciated the eco-friendly approach and the opportunity to explore the beautiful rice paddies and surrounding villages. The hands-on activities and the warm hospitality of the host family made it a memorable stay.

Accommodation Tips

What to Look For: Choosing the right accommodation can greatly enhance your travel experience. Here are some key factors to consider when selecting a place to stay in Vietnam:

Location: Consider the proximity of the accommodation to key attractions, public transportation, restaurants, and shopping areas. Staying in a central location can save time and make it easier to explore the city.

Amenities: Look for accommodations that offer the amenities you need for a comfortable stay. Common amenities include WiFi, air conditioning, on-site dining, fitness centers, swimming pools, and laundry services.

Reviews: Read reviews from other travelers to get an idea of the quality and service of the accommodation. Websites like TripAdvisor, Booking.com, and Google Reviews can provide valuable insights.

Safety and Cleanliness: Ensure that the accommodation follows proper safety and hygiene practices. Check for information on cleanliness protocols and guest safety measures.

Price: Compare prices across different accommodations to find the best value for your budget. Consider any additional fees or charges that may apply.

Special Features: Some accommodations offer unique features, such as cultural workshops, guided tours, or eco-friendly practices. If you're looking for a special experience, check for these offerings.

Budgeting for Accommodation:

Budgeting for accommodation is an essential part of trip planning. Here are some tips to help you manage your accommodation expenses in Vietnam:

Set a Budget: Determine how much you're willing to spend on accommodation per night and for the entire trip. This will help you narrow down your options and avoid overspending.

Research and Compare: Take the time to research different accommodations and compare prices. Use booking platforms and travel websites to find deals and discounts.

Consider Different Types of Accommodations: Depending on your budget, consider a mix of luxury hotels, mid-range hotels, boutique hotels, guesthouses, hostels, and homestays. This can help you balance comfort and cost.

Book in Advance: Booking your accommodation in advance can often result in better prices and availability. Look for early booking discounts and special offers.

Flexible Dates: If your travel dates are flexible, consider staying during off-peak seasons when accommodation prices are lower. Avoiding weekends and holidays can also help reduce costs.

Look for Package Deals: Some travel websites and tour operators offer package deals that include accommodation, transportation, and activities. These can provide good value for money.

Negotiate: In some cases, especially for longer stays or last-minute bookings, you may be able to negotiate a better rate directly with the accommodation.

Read the Fine Print: Be aware of any additional fees, such as resort fees, taxes, or charges for extra services. Factor these into your budget to avoid surprises.

By considering these factors and tips, you can find the right accommodation that fits your needs and budget, ensuring a comfortable and enjoyable stay in Vietnam.

Getting Around Vietnam

Vietnam is a country with a well-developed transportation network, making it easy for travelers to explore its diverse landscapes, bustling cities, and charming towns. Whether you prefer to fly, take the train, or use local buses and taxis, there are numerous options to suit your travel style and budget. In this chapter, we'll explore the various modes of transportation available in Vietnam, including domestic flights, trains, buses, and taxis, to help you navigate the country efficiently and comfortably.

Domestic Flights

Description: Domestic flights are a convenient and time-saving option for traveling between major cities and regions in Vietnam. The country has a number of well-connected airports, and several airlines operate frequent domestic flights, making it easy to cover long distances quickly.

Major Airlines:
- **Vietnam Airlines**: The national carrier, offering a wide range of domestic flights with excellent service.
- **VietJet Air:** A popular low-cost airline known for its affordable fares and extensive route network.
- **Bamboo Airways**: A relatively new airline offering competitive prices and a growing number of domestic routes.
- **Jetstar Pacific**: Another low-cost airline providing budget-friendly options for domestic travel.

Key Airports:
- Noi Bai International Airport (Hanoi)
- Tan Son Nhat International Airport (Ho Chi Minh City)
- Da Nang International Airport (Da Nang)
- Cam Ranh International Airport (Nha Trang)
- Phu Quoc International Airport (Phu Quoc Island)

Highlights:
- **Time-Saving:** Domestic flights are the fastest way to travel between distant cities and regions.
- **Extensive Network**: Frequent flights connecting major cities and tourist destinations.
- **Competitive Pricing**: Multiple airlines offering a range of fares to suit different budgets.

What to Expect:
- **Booking:** Flights can be booked online through airline websites or travel

agencies. It's advisable to book in advance for the best deals.
- **Check-In**: Arrive at the airport at least 1-2 hours before your flight for check-in and security procedures.
- **Baggage**: Be aware of baggage allowances and fees for excess luggage, especially on low-cost airlines.
- **Onboard Service**: Depending on the airline, you can expect varying levels of in-flight service, from basic refreshments to full meals.

Pricing:
- Flights between major cities like Hanoi and Ho Chi Minh City typically range from $50 to $150 USD one-way, depending on the airline and booking time.
- Shorter flights, such as those between Da Nang and Ho Chi Minh City, can range from $30 to $100 USD one-way.

Flying with Vietnam Airlines from Hanoi to Ho Chi Minh City was a smooth and pleasant experience. The service was excellent, and the flight was on time. VietJet Air provided an affordable and efficient option for a short flight from Da Nang to Ho Chi Minh City, although the check-in process was a bit crowded. Bamboo Airways impressed me with its modern aircraft and friendly staff on a flight from Hanoi to Phu Quoc Island.

Trains and Rail Travel

Description: Train travel in Vietnam offers a scenic and comfortable way to explore the country, with routes connecting major cities and regions. The Reunification Express, running from Hanoi to Ho Chi Minh City, is the most famous route, offering a unique perspective of Vietnam's landscapes and culture.

Main Routes:
- **Hanoi to Ho Chi Minh City**: The Reunification Express, covering a distance of over 1,700 kilometers, with several stops along the way.
- **Hanoi to Sapa (Lao Cai):** A popular route for travelers visiting the mountainous region of Sapa.
- Hanoi to Da Nang/Hue: A scenic route along the central coast, passing through beautiful landscapes and coastal towns.

Classes of Service:
- **Soft Sleeper**: Comfortable compartments with four berths, providing a good night's sleep on long journeys.
- **Hard Sleeper**: Compartments with six berths, offering a more budget-friendly option.
- **Soft Seat:** Comfortable seating for shorter journeys.
- **Hard Seat**: Basic seating for budget travelers.

Highlights:
- **Scenic Journeys:** Enjoy breathtaking views of the countryside, mountains, and coastline.
- **Comfortable Travel:** Spacious compartments and sleeping berths for overnight journeys.
- **Cultural Experience**: Interact with locals and fellow travelers, gaining insights into Vietnamese culture.

What to Expect:
- **Booking**: Train tickets can be booked online, at railway stations, or through travel agencies. It's advisable to book in advance for popular routes.
- **Travel Time**: Train journeys can be long, so be prepared for extended travel times, especially on routes like Hanoi to Ho Chi Minh City.
- **Amenities**: Onboard amenities vary, with some trains offering dining cars, restrooms, and charging points.

Pricing:
- Soft Sleeper tickets for the Hanoi to Ho Chi Minh City route typically range from $70 to $100 USD one-way.
- Hard Sleeper tickets for the same route range from $50 to $80 USD one-way.
- Soft Seat tickets for shorter routes, such as Hanoi to Da Nang, range from $40 to $60 USD one-way.

Taking the Reunification Express from Hanoi to Da Nang was a memorable experience. The scenic views along the coast and the comfortable soft sleeper compartment made the journey enjoyable. The overnight train from Hanoi to Sapa was another highlight, with stunning views of the mountains and a cozy sleeping berth.

Buses and Coaches

Description: Buses and coaches are a popular and cost-effective way to travel around Vietnam. The country has an extensive network of bus routes connecting cities, towns, and tourist destinations. Both local buses and long-distance coaches are available, offering various levels of comfort and convenience.

Types of Buses:
- **Local Buses**: Budget-friendly options for short journeys within cities and towns.
- **Long-Distance Coaches**: Comfortable coaches for longer journeys between cities and regions, often equipped with reclining seats and air conditioning.
- **Sleeper Buses**: Long-distance coaches with sleeping berths for overnight travel, providing a budget-friendly alternative to trains.

Major Bus Companies:
- **Sinh Tourist**: A well-known company offering comfortable coaches and organized tours.
- **Futa Bus Lines**: A popular choice for long-distance travel, known for its reliable service and modern fleet.
- **Hoang Long**: Another reputable company offering long-distance bus services with comfortable amenities.

Highlights:
- **Cost-Effective:** Buses and coaches are an affordable way to travel around Vietnam.
- **Extensive Network**: Comprehensive coverage of cities, towns, and tourist destinations.
- **Variety of Options**: Different types of buses and coaches to suit various budgets and travel preferences.

What to Expect:

- **Booking**: Tickets can be purchased online, at bus stations, or through travel agencies. It's advisable to book in advance for long-distance journeys.
- **Travel Time:** Be prepared for potentially long travel times, especially on long-distance routes.
- **Amenities**: Long-distance coaches and sleeper buses typically offer comfortable seating or sleeping berths, air conditioning, and restrooms.

Pricing:
- Sleeper bus tickets for long-distance routes like Ho Chi Minh City to Nha Trang range from $15 to $30 USD one-way.
- Long-distance coach tickets for routes like Hanoi to Ha Long Bay range from $10 to $20 USD one-way.

Traveling by sleeper bus from Ho Chi Minh City to Nha Trang was a budget-friendly and comfortable experience. The sleeping berth allowed me to rest during the overnight journey, and the bus arrived on time. Using Sinh Tourist for a coach trip from Hanoi to Ha Long Bay was convenient, with comfortable seats and friendly service.

Taxis and Ride-Sharing Services

Description: Taxis and ride-sharing services are widely available in Vietnam, providing convenient transportation options for short trips within cities and towns. They are ideal for getting around urban areas, reaching specific destinations, or traveling to and from airports.

Taxi Companies:

- **Mai Linh Taxi:** A reputable company offering reliable service with metered fares.
- **Vinasun Taxi**: Another well-known company with a large fleet and transparent pricing.

Ride-Sharing Services:
- **Grab:** The most popular ride-sharing app in Vietnam, offering convenient and affordable transportation options. Grab also provides motorbike taxis (GrabBike) for quick and budget-friendly rides.

Highlights:
- **Convenience**: Easily accessible transportation options for short trips within cities and towns.
- **Flexibility**: Taxis and ride-sharing services can be hailed on the street, booked through apps, or arranged in advance.
- **Variety**: Options for both car and motorbike taxis, catering to different preferences and budgets.

What to Expect:
- **Booking**: Taxis can be hailed on the street or booked through hotel reception. Ride-sharing services like Grab can be booked through mobile apps.
- **Fares**: Metered fares for taxis and transparent pricing for ride-sharing services. Ride-sharing apps often provide fare estimates before booking.
- **Service Quality**: Reputable taxi companies and ride-sharing services offer reliable and professional service.

Be sure to check for driver ratings and reviews on ride-sharing apps.

Pricing:
- Short taxi rides within cities typically cost between $2 to $5 USD, depending on the distance and traffic conditions.
- Ride-sharing services like Grab offer competitive pricing, with motorbike taxi rides starting at around $1 USD and car rides starting at around $2 to $3 USD for short distances.

Using Grab in Ho Chi Minh City was incredibly convenient, with quick response times and affordable fares. The motorbike taxi option (GrabBike) was particularly useful for navigating through the city's traffic. Mai Linh Taxi provided reliable service with metered fares during my stay in Hanoi, and the drivers were friendly and knowledgeable. Vinasun Taxi was another trustworthy option for short trips within the city.

Chapter 4: Transportation

Travel Tips

Navigating Public Transportation

Public transportation in Vietnam is an efficient and cost-effective way to explore cities and towns. Here are some tips to help you navigate public transportation with ease:

Research Routes and Schedules: Before using public transportation, familiarize yourself with the routes and schedules. Many cities have bus routes and schedules available online or through mobile apps. Knowing which bus or train to take and when it arrives will save you time and make your journey smoother.

Use Transportation Apps: Apps like Grab and Moovit can help you find the best routes, provide real-time updates, and even offer ride-sharing options. These apps are especially useful for navigating busy cities like Hanoi and Ho Chi Minh City.

Have Small Change Ready: When using buses or local transportation, it's helpful to have small change or local currency on hand to pay for fares. Many buses only accept cash, and having the exact fare will make the process easier.

Be Prepared for Crowds: Public transportation in Vietnam, especially in major cities, can be crowded during peak hours. Be prepared for busy buses and trains, and consider traveling during off-peak times if you prefer a more relaxed journey.

Respect Local Customs: While using public transportation, be mindful of local customs and etiquette. Offer your seat to elderly passengers, avoid loud conversations, and follow any posted rules or guidelines.

Plan for Transfers: If your journey requires transferring between different modes of transportation, plan your route in advance and allow extra time for transfers. Knowing where to switch buses or trains will help you avoid confusion and delays.

Using public buses in Hanoi was a convenient and affordable way to explore the city. The bus routes were well-marked, and the locals were helpful in guiding me to the right bus. In Ho Chi Minh City, the Grab app was incredibly useful for finding the quickest routes and booking rides. The real-time updates and fare estimates made navigating the city a breeze.

Renting Vehicles

Renting a vehicle in Vietnam can give you the freedom to explore at your own pace, especially in areas with limited public transportation. Here are some tips for renting vehicles in Vietnam:

Choose the Right Vehicle: Depending on your travel plans, you can rent a car, motorbike, or bicycle. Motorbikes are popular for short trips and exploring rural areas, while cars are ideal for longer journeys and traveling with family or friends.

Check Rental Requirements: To rent a vehicle in Vietnam, you'll need a valid driver's license. For motorbikes, an International Driving Permit (IDP) with a motorcycle endorsement is often required. Make sure to check the rental company's requirements and have the necessary documents.

Inspect the Vehicle: Before renting, thoroughly inspect the vehicle for any existing damage and ensure it's in good working condition. Take photos or videos of the vehicle's condition to avoid any disputes when returning it.

Understand the Rental Agreement: Carefully read the rental agreement and understand the terms and conditions, including insurance coverage, mileage limits, and fuel policies. Ask the rental company about any additional fees or charges.

Wear Safety Gear: If you're renting a motorbike, always wear a helmet and appropriate safety gear. Helmets are mandatory in Vietnam, and wearing protective clothing can enhance your safety on the road.

Plan Your Route: Plan your route in advance and use navigation apps like Google Maps for directions. Be aware of road conditions, traffic rules, and any potential hazards.

Drive Cautiously: Traffic in Vietnam can be chaotic, especially in cities. Drive cautiously, follow traffic rules, and be mindful of other road users. Avoid driving at night in unfamiliar areas.

Renting a motorbike in Hoi An allowed me to explore the countryside and visit nearby attractions at my own pace. The rental process was straightforward, and the rental company provided a well-maintained bike and a helmet. In Da Nang, renting a car was a great option for a family trip, providing comfort and convenience for longer journeys. The car rental company offered comprehensive insurance coverage and clear rental terms, making the experience hassle-free.

Vietnamese Cuisine

Vietnamese cuisine is renowned for its vibrant flavors, fresh ingredients, and diverse dishes. With influences from China, France, and neighboring countries, Vietnamese food offers a unique blend of flavors and textures. From savory street food to hearty traditional dishes, there's something to delight every palate. In this chapter, we'll explore must-try dishes, street food delights, and dining etiquette to help you fully enjoy the culinary delights of Vietnam.

Must-Try Dishes

Description: Vietnam is home to a wide variety of delicious dishes that showcase the country's culinary diversity. Here are some must-try dishes that you shouldn't miss during your visit:

Examples of Must-Try Dishes:
1. **Pho:** A quintessential Vietnamese dish, pho is a fragrant noodle soup made with beef or chicken, fresh herbs, and rice noodles. It's often enjoyed as a breakfast dish but can be eaten any time of day.

2. **Banh Mi:** A Vietnamese sandwich that combines French baguettes with various fillings, such as grilled pork, pate, pickled vegetables, and fresh herbs. It's a popular street food that offers a delightful mix of flavors and textures.

3. **Bun Cha**: A dish originating from Hanoi, bun cha consists of grilled pork patties and pork belly served with vermicelli noodles, fresh herbs, and a dipping sauce. It's a flavorful and satisfying meal.

4. **Goi Cuon (Spring Rolls):** Fresh spring rolls made with rice paper, shrimp or pork, vermicelli noodles, and fresh herbs. They're typically served with a peanut dipping sauce and make for a light and refreshing appetizer.

5. **Com Tam (Broken Rice):** A popular dish in southern Vietnam, com tam features broken rice grains served with grilled pork, pickled vegetables, and a fried egg. It's often topped with scallions and served with a side of fish sauce.

Highlights:
- **Flavorful and Fresh**: Vietnamese dishes are known for their fresh

ingredients and balanced flavors, often combining savory, sweet, sour, and spicy elements.
- **Diverse Options**: From soups and sandwiches to noodles and rice dishes, there's a wide variety of options to suit different tastes.
- **Cultural Significance**: Many dishes have regional variations and cultural significance, offering insights into the local traditions and history.

What to Expect:
- **Fresh Ingredients**: Expect dishes made with fresh herbs, vegetables, and high-quality meats.
- **Aromatic Flavors**: Vietnamese cuisine often features aromatic flavors from ingredients like lemongrass, basil, mint, and coriander.
- **Light and Healthy**: Many Vietnamese dishes are light and healthy, with a focus on fresh produce and minimal use of oil and fat.

Enjoying a bowl of pho at a local eatery in Hanoi was a memorable experience. The rich broth, tender beef, and fragrant herbs made it a comforting and delicious meal. Trying banh mi from a street vendor in Ho Chi Minh City was another highlight. The crispy baguette and flavorful fillings created a perfect harmony of tastes and textures. In Hanoi, I had the chance to try bun cha, and the combination of grilled pork, noodles, and fresh herbs was incredibly satisfying. Goi cuon provided a refreshing and light appetizer, while com tam in Ho Chi Minh City offered a hearty and flavorful meal.

Street Food Delights

Description: Vietnam is famous for its vibrant street food culture, with bustling markets and food stalls offering a wide variety of delicious and affordable dishes. Exploring the street food scene is a must for any visitor, as it provides an authentic taste of local flavors and culinary traditions.

Examples of Street Food Delights:
1. **Banh Xeo (Vietnamese Pancakes):** Savory pancakes made with rice flour, turmeric, and coconut milk, filled with shrimp, pork, and bean sprouts. They're served with fresh herbs and a dipping sauce.

2. **Bun Bo Hue:** A spicy and flavorful noodle soup from Hue, made with beef, lemongrass, and rice noodles. It's known for its rich and aromatic broth.

3. **Che (Vietnamese Dessert):** A variety of sweet desserts made with ingredients like beans, coconut milk, and jelly. Che can be

served hot or cold and comes in many different variations.

4. **Nem Nuong (Grilled Pork Sausages):** Grilled pork sausages served with rice paper, fresh herbs, and a dipping sauce. They're a popular street food snack that's both flavorful and satisfying.

5. **Ca Phe Sua Da (Vietnamese Iced Coffee):** Strong and aromatic coffee brewed with a drip filter, mixed with sweetened condensed milk, and served over ice. It's a refreshing and invigorating drink, perfect for hot days.

Highlights:
- **Affordable and Delicious:** Street food in Vietnam is not only delicious but also budget-friendly, making it accessible to everyone.
- **Authentic Experience**: Sampling street food allows you to experience the local culture and culinary traditions firsthand.
- **Wide Variety**: From savory snacks to sweet treats, there's a diverse range of street food options to try.

What to Expect:
- **Bustling Atmosphere:** Street food stalls and markets are often lively and busy, with locals and tourists alike enjoying the delicious offerings.
- **Fresh and Flavorful**: Street food dishes are made with fresh ingredients and packed with bold flavors.
- **Casual Dining**: Enjoying street food is a casual and relaxed experience, often eaten while standing or sitting on small stools.

Trying banh xeo at a street food market in Da Nang was a delightful experience. The crispy pancake and savory fillings were a perfect combination. Bun bo hue in Hue provided a spicy and aromatic noodle soup that warmed me up on a cool evening. Sampling different varieties of che at a dessert stall in Ho Chi Minh City was a sweet and enjoyable treat. Nem nuong from a street vendor in Nha Trang was flavorful and satisfying, while ca phe sua da offered a refreshing pick-me-up during my explorations in Hanoi.

Dining Etiquette

Description: Understanding dining etiquette is important when enjoying meals in Vietnam, as it shows respect for the local culture and traditions.

Here are some key points to keep in mind:
- **Use of Chopsticks**: Chopsticks are commonly used in Vietnamese dining. When not in use, place them neatly on the chopstick rest or across your bowl. Avoid sticking them upright in a bowl of rice, as this resembles a funeral offering.
- **Sharing Dishes:** Meals are often served family-style, with shared dishes placed in the center of the table. It's polite to take small portions and avoid reaching across the table.
- **Eating Noodles**: When eating noodle dishes like pho, it's acceptable to lift the bowl to your mouth and use chopsticks to guide the noodles. Drinking directly from the bowl is also common.

- **Respectful Behavior**: Show respect to the host and elders by waiting for them to start eating first. Express gratitude for the meal by saying "Cảm ơn" (Thank you) to the host or server.
- **Handling Bowls and Plates**: Hold bowls close to your mouth when eating, especially for rice and noodle dishes. Avoid leaving chopsticks or utensils sticking out of the dishes.

Highlights:
- **Respectful Dining**: Following dining etiquette shows respect for the local culture and enhances your dining experience.
- **Family-Style Meals**: Sharing dishes fosters a sense of community and allows you to try a variety of foods.
- **Proper Use of Utensils**: Using chopsticks and handling bowls correctly is an important part of Vietnamese dining etiquette.

What to Expect:
- **Warm Hospitality**: Vietnamese hosts are known for their warm hospitality and generosity. Showing appreciation and gratitude is always appreciated.
- **Casual Atmosphere**: Dining in Vietnam is often a casual and relaxed affair, with a focus on enjoying the food and company.
- **Cultural Traditions**: Participating in dining traditions and etiquette provides a deeper understanding of Vietnamese culture.

During my travels in Vietnam, I found that observing dining etiquette added to the enjoyment of my meals. Using chopsticks and sharing dishes with others created a sense of camaraderie and allowed me to try a variety of flavors. Expressing gratitude to my hosts and servers was always met with warm smiles and appreciation. Dining with locals gave me valuable insights into Vietnamese culture and traditions, making each meal a memorable experience.

Drinks and Nightlife

Vietnam boasts a vibrant drinks and nightlife scene, offering a variety of popular beverages and exciting venues to enjoy after dark. Whether you're looking for a refreshing local drink, a cozy bar to unwind, or a lively nightclub to dance the night away, Vietnam has something for everyone. In this section, we'll explore popular beverages, the best bars and nightclubs, and local etiquette to help you make the most of Vietnam's nightlife.

Popular Beverages

Description: Vietnamese beverages are known for their unique flavors and refreshing qualities. Here are some popular drinks you should try during your visit:

Examples of Popular Beverages:
1. **Ca Phe Sua Da (Vietnamese Iced Coffee)**: Strong and aromatic coffee brewed with a drip filter, mixed with sweetened condensed milk, and served over ice. It's a refreshing and invigorating drink, perfect for hot days.

2. **Tra Da (Iced Tea)**: A light and refreshing iced tea commonly served in local restaurants and street food stalls. It's often unsweetened and provides a cool and hydrating option.

3. **Nuoc Mia (Sugarcane Juice):** Freshly pressed sugarcane juice, typically served over ice with a splash of lime. It's a sweet and revitalizing drink, popular in the hot climate.

4. **Sinh To (Fruit Smoothies):** Delicious and healthy fruit smoothies made with fresh tropical fruits, such as mango, papaya, dragon fruit, and avocado. They're often blended with milk or yogurt.

5. **Bia Hoi (Fresh Beer):** A light and refreshing draft beer that's brewed daily and served in small, local bars. Bia hoi is an iconic part of Vietnamese drinking culture and is enjoyed by locals and tourists alike.

Highlights:
- **Refreshing and Flavorful**: Vietnamese beverages are known for their refreshing qualities and bold flavors.
- **Unique Ingredients**: Many drinks feature unique local ingredients, such as condensed milk, sugarcane, and tropical fruits.
- **Cultural Experience**: Trying local beverages provides a taste of Vietnamese culture and culinary traditions.

What to Expect:
- **Fresh Ingredients**: Drinks made with fresh, high-quality ingredients for the best taste and experience.
- **Variety of Options**: A wide range of beverages to suit different preferences, from coffee and tea to fruit smoothies and beer.
- **Affordable Prices**: Most beverages are budget-friendly, making it easy to try a variety of drinks without breaking the bank.

Enjoying ca phe sua da at a local cafe in Hanoi was a highlight of my trip. The strong coffee and sweet condensed milk created a perfect balance of flavors. Trying nuoc mia from a street vendor in Ho Chi Minh City was a refreshing treat on a hot day, and the addition of lime added a nice tangy twist. Sinh to made with fresh mango and yogurt was a delicious and healthy option that I enjoyed during my time in Da Nang. Bia hoi provided a fun and social experience in Hanoi, where I joined locals and fellow travelers for a cold beer at a bustling street corner.

Best Bars and Nightclubs

Description: Vietnam's nightlife scene offers a diverse range of bars and nightclubs, from chic rooftop bars with stunning views to lively clubs with energetic dance floors. Whether you're looking for a relaxed evening with friends or a night of dancing and entertainment, there's something to suit every mood.

Examples of Best Bars and Nightclubs:

1. **Bia Hoi Junction (Hanoi):**
   - Located in the heart of Hanoi's Old Quarter, Bia Hoi Junction is a lively spot where locals and tourists gather to enjoy fresh beer and street food in a vibrant atmosphere.

2. **Rex Hotel Rooftop Bar (Ho Chi Minh City):** A historic and elegant rooftop bar offering panoramic views of the city skyline. It's a perfect place to unwind with a cocktail and enjoy live music.

3. **Sky36 (Da Nang):** One of the highest rooftop bars in Vietnam, Sky36 offers stunning views of Da Nang, a stylish setting, and a mix of live DJ performances and dance music.

4. **Dive Bar (Hoi An):** A popular bar in Hoi An with a relaxed vibe, live music, and a great selection of cocktails and craft beers. It's a favorite hangout for both locals and travelers.

5. **Lush Nightclub (Ho Chi Minh City):** A trendy nightclub known for its energetic atmosphere, international DJs, and lively dance floor. It's a go-to destination for a night of dancing and entertainment.

Highlights:
- **Variety of Venues:** From rooftop bars with breathtaking views to lively nightclubs with dance floors, there's a diverse range of nightlife options.
- **Vibrant Atmosphere**: Enjoy the lively and energetic vibe of Vietnam's nightlife scene, with venues catering to different tastes and preferences.
- **Live Music and Entertainment**: Many bars and clubs offer live music, DJ performances, and entertainment to enhance your night out.

What to Expect:
- **Stunning Views:** Rooftop bars often provide panoramic views of the city skyline or coastline, creating a memorable backdrop for your evening.
- **Lively Crowds**: Nightclubs and popular bars can get busy, especially on weekends, with a mix of locals and tourists enjoying the nightlife.
- **Varied Drink Menus**: Expect a wide selection of drinks, including cocktails, craft beers, wines, and spirits, often accompanied by light snacks or appetizers.

Visiting Bia Hoi Junction in Hanoi was a fun and lively experience. The bustling atmosphere, friendly locals, and affordable beer made it a great spot to unwind after a day of sightseeing. The rooftop bar at the Rex Hotel in Ho Chi Minh City offered a more elegant setting, with stunning views of the city and live music creating a relaxed ambiance. Sky36 in Da Nang provided an unforgettable experience with its stylish decor, breathtaking views, and energetic DJ performances. Dive Bar in Hoi An was a favorite hangout, with its laid-back vibe and excellent live music. Lush Nightclub in Ho Chi Minh City delivered an exciting night of dancing and entertainment, with a vibrant atmosphere and top-notch DJ sets.

Local Etiquette

Description: Understanding local etiquette is important when enjoying drinks and nightlife in Vietnam.

Here are some key points to keep in mind to ensure a respectful and enjoyable experience:

- **Cheers and Toasting**: When drinking with locals, it's common to raise your glass and say "Mot, Hai, Ba, Yo!" (One, Two, Three, Cheers!) before taking a sip. This is a fun and social way to bond with others.
- **Respect for Elders**: Show respect to older individuals by inviting them to drink first and waiting for them to start before you take a sip. This gesture demonstrates politeness and respect for age and seniority.
- **Pacing Yourself**: Vietnamese drinking culture often involves multiple rounds of toasts and cheers. Pace yourself and enjoy the social aspect of drinking rather than consuming large quantities quickly.
- **Using Two Hands**: When offering or receiving a drink, use both hands as a sign of respect. This is particularly important when serving or receiving from someone older or of higher status.
- **Moderation**: While enjoying drinks and nightlife, it's important to drink responsibly and avoid excessive consumption. Be mindful of your limits and ensure a safe and enjoyable evening for yourself and others.

Highlights:
- **Social Bonding**: Drinking and toasting are important social activities in Vietnamese culture, fostering connections and camaraderie.
- **Polite Gestures**: Following local etiquette and showing respect enhances your interactions and experiences with locals.
- **Enjoying the Moment**: Emphasize the social and enjoyable aspects of drinking rather than focusing on consuming large quantities.

What to Expect:
- **Friendly Atmosphere**: Vietnamese people are known for their friendliness and hospitality, making for a welcoming nightlife experience.
- **Cultural Traditions**: Participating in toasts and drinking customs provides insights into Vietnamese culture and traditions.
- **Relaxed Vibe**: While enjoying drinks, the focus is often on socializing, sharing stories, and having a good time with friends and new acquaintances.

Joining locals for a drink at Bia Hoi Junction in Hanoi was a memorable experience. The friendly atmosphere and shared toasts created a sense of camaraderie and connection. Observing local etiquette, such as using both hands to receive a drink and respecting elders, added to the enjoyment of the evening. At the rooftop bar in the Rex Hotel, the elegant setting and live music provided a perfect backdrop for a relaxed and enjoyable evening. Participating in toasts and bonding with fellow travelers at Dive Bar in Hoi An made for a fun and memorable night out.

Chapter 6: Activities and Adventures

Outdoor Adventures

Vietnam is a paradise for outdoor enthusiasts, offering a wide range of activities and adventures that allow travelers to explore its stunning landscapes and natural beauty. From hiking through lush mountains to enjoying water sports on pristine beaches, Vietnam's diverse terrain provides endless opportunities for adventure. In this section, we'll explore hiking and trekking, water sports, and cycling tours to help you make the most of your outdoor adventures in Vietnam.

Hiking and Trekking

Description: Hiking and trekking are popular activities in Vietnam, allowing travelers to explore the country's diverse landscapes, from terraced rice fields to rugged mountains and dense forests. Whether you're an experienced trekker or a casual hiker, there are trails and routes to suit all levels of fitness and experience.

Examples of Hiking and Trekking Destinations:

1. **Sapa:** Located in the northern region, Sapa is renowned for its terraced rice fields, ethnic minority villages, and stunning mountain views. Popular trekking routes include the hike to Fansipan, the highest peak in Indochina, and treks through the Muong Hoa Valley.

2. **Mai Chau**: A peaceful valley surrounded by rice paddies and limestone mountains, Mai Chau offers scenic hikes through local villages and beautiful countryside. The Pu Luong Nature Reserve is a popular trekking destination in the area.

3. **Phong Nha-Ke Bang National Park**: Known for its impressive cave systems and karst landscapes, this national park offers a variety of trekking routes, including hikes to the famous Son Doong Cave and Paradise Cave.

4. **Cat Ba Island**: Located in Ha Long Bay, Cat Ba Island offers hiking trails through Cat Ba National Park, where you can explore dense forests, limestone hills, and scenic viewpoints.

5. **Ba Be National Park**: A remote and picturesque park in northern Vietnam, Ba Be offers trekking routes through lush forests, ethnic minority villages, and along the shores of Ba Be Lake.

Highlights:
- **Scenic Landscapes:** Enjoy breathtaking views of rice terraces, mountains, forests, and valleys.
- **Cultural Encounters:** Interact with local ethnic minority communities and learn about their traditions and way of life.
- **Diverse Terrain:** Experience a variety of terrains, from challenging mountain hikes to gentle walks through picturesque valleys.

What to Expect:
- **Preparation**: Wear comfortable hiking shoes, bring plenty of water, and pack essentials like a hat, sunscreen, and insect repellent.
- **Guided Tours:** Consider joining guided trekking tours for a safer and more informative experience, especially in remote areas.
- **Fitness Levels:** Choose hiking and trekking routes that match your fitness level and experience.

Trekking in Sapa was a highlight of my trip. The stunning terraced rice fields and the warm hospitality of the ethnic minority villages made the experience unforgettable. Hiking through Phong Nha-Ke Bang National Park and exploring its magnificent caves was a thrilling adventure. The dense forests and limestone hills of Cat Ba Island provided a scenic and enjoyable hiking experience.

Water Sports

Description: Vietnam's beautiful coastline, rivers, and lakes offer a wide range of water sports and activities for adventure seekers. From kayaking in scenic bays to scuba diving in coral reefs, there are plenty of opportunities to enjoy the water and explore Vietnam's marine and aquatic environments.

Examples of Water Sports Destinations:

1. **Ha Long Bay**: A UNESCO World Heritage Site known for its emerald waters and limestone karsts, Ha Long Bay is a popular destination for kayaking, sailing, and boat tours.

2. **Nha Trang**: A coastal city with stunning beaches and vibrant coral reefs, Nha Trang is perfect for snorkeling, scuba diving, and jet skiing.

3. **Phu Quoc Island:** An island paradise with clear waters and abundant marine life, Phu Quoc offers excellent snorkeling and diving opportunities, as well as fishing and sailing.
4. **Mui Ne:** Known for its sandy beaches and strong winds, Mui Ne is a hotspot for kite surfing, windsurfing, and paddleboarding.
5. **Mekong Delta**: Explore the intricate network of rivers and canals in the Mekong Delta by taking boat tours, kayaking, or even participating in traditional fishing activities.

Highlights:
- **Adventure and Excitement:** Engage in thrilling water sports activities, from diving and snorkeling to kite surfing and jet skiing.
- **Marine Life:** Discover vibrant coral reefs and diverse marine life in some of Vietnam's best diving and snorkeling spots.
- **Scenic Waterways**: Enjoy the natural beauty of Vietnam's coastal regions, bays, and rivers through various water-based activities.

What to Expect:
- **Equipment:** Rent or bring your own water sports equipment, such as kayaks, snorkeling gear, or diving equipment. Many tour operators provide rentals and guided activities.
- **Safety**: Follow safety guidelines and instructions from instructors or guides, especially for activities like scuba diving and kite surfing.
- **Skill Levels**: Choose water sports activities that match your skill level and experience. Many destinations offer beginner lessons and guided tours.

Kayaking in Ha Long Bay was an incredible experience. Paddling through the emerald waters and exploring hidden caves and lagoons was both peaceful and exhilarating. Snorkeling in Nha Trang revealed vibrant coral reefs and diverse marine life, making it a memorable underwater adventure. Kite surfing in Mui Ne was a thrilling activity, with the strong winds and sandy beaches providing the perfect conditions for this exciting sport.

Cycling Tours

Description: Cycling tours are a fantastic way to explore Vietnam's scenic landscapes, rural villages, and bustling cities. Whether you're cycling through the countryside or navigating the streets of vibrant cities, biking allows you to experience the sights, sounds, and culture of Vietnam up close.

Examples of Cycling Tour Destinations:
1. **Hoi An:** Known for its well-preserved ancient town and beautiful countryside, Hoi An offers scenic cycling routes through rice paddies, local villages, and along the Thu Bon River.
2. **Mekong Delta:** Explore the Mekong Delta's intricate network of canals, orchards, and rural villages by bike. Cycling tours provide an immersive experience of the delta's unique landscape and way of life.
3. **Hanoi**: Discover the charm of Hanoi's Old Quarter and its surrounding areas on a cycling tour. Navigate the bustling streets, historic sites, and peaceful lakes by bike.
4. **Sapa**: Cycle through the stunning landscapes of Sapa, with routes that take you

through terraced rice fields, ethnic minority villages, and mountain trails.

5. **Da Lat**: Known for its cool climate and beautiful scenery, Da Lat offers cycling routes through pine forests, flower gardens, and rolling hills.

Highlights:
- **Scenic Routes:** Enjoy breathtaking views and diverse landscapes while cycling through Vietnam's countryside, cities, and coastal regions.
- **Cultural Encounters:** Interact with locals, visit traditional villages, and learn about the local way of life during your cycling tours.
- **Fitness and Adventure**: Cycling tours provide a healthy and active way to explore Vietnam, suitable for various fitness levels and interests.

What to Expect:
- **Bike Rentals:** Rent a bike from local shops or tour operators. Make sure the bike is in good condition and suitable for the terrain you'll be cycling on.
- **Guided Tours:** Consider joining guided cycling tours for a more informative and organized experience. Guides can provide insights into the area's history, culture, and attractions.
- **Safety Gear**: Wear appropriate safety gear, including a helmet, and follow local traffic rules and regulations. Bring water, sunscreen, and a map or GPS device.

Cycling through the countryside of Hoi An was a highlight of my trip. The scenic routes, friendly locals, and peaceful atmosphere made it a delightful experience. Exploring the Mekong Delta by bike allowed me to see the rural landscape up close and interact with local villagers. Cycling around Hanoi's Old Quarter provided a unique perspective of the city's historic sites and vibrant streets. The cool climate and beautiful scenery of Da Lat made it an ideal destination for a relaxing and enjoyable cycling tour.

Chapter 7: Activities and Adventures

Cultural Experiences

Vietnam is a country rich in cultural heritage, with a long history and diverse traditions. Exploring cultural experiences in Vietnam allows travelers to immerse themselves in the local way of life, learn about the country's history, and participate in traditional activities. In this section, we'll explore visiting temples and pagodas, traditional performances, and festivals and celebrations to help you fully experience the cultural richness of Vietnam.

Visiting Temples and Pagodas

Description: Temples and pagodas are an integral part of Vietnamese culture and spirituality. These sacred sites are not only places of worship but also architectural masterpieces that reflect the country's rich history and religious traditions. Visiting temples and pagodas offers a glimpse into the spiritual life of the Vietnamese people and provides an opportunity to admire their beautiful architecture and serene surroundings.

Examples of Temples and Pagodas:
1. **Tran Quoc Pagoda (Hanoi):**
   - Located on an island in West Lake, Tran Quoc Pagoda is the oldest Buddhist temple in Hanoi. It features a serene setting, ancient stupas, and beautiful gardens.

2. **Thien Mu Pagoda (Hue):**
   - Situated on a hill overlooking the Perfume River, Thien Mu Pagoda is a symbol of Hue and one of the most iconic religious sites in Vietnam. The pagoda's seven-story tower and peaceful gardens make it a must-visit destination.

3. **Bai Dinh Pagoda (Ninh Binh):**
   - The largest pagoda complex in Vietnam, Bai Dinh Pagoda is known for its impressive scale, stunning architecture, and numerous statues of Buddha. It's a major pilgrimage site for Buddhists.

4. **Jade Emperor Pagoda (Ho Chi Minh City):**
   - A vibrant Taoist temple in the heart of the city, Jade Emperor Pagoda is dedicated to the Jade Emperor and features intricate carvings, statues, and altars.

5. **One Pillar Pagoda (Hanoi):**
   - A unique pagoda built on a single stone pillar, One Pillar Pagoda is an iconic symbol of Hanoi and a testament to the ingenuity of Vietnamese architecture.

Highlights:
- **Architectural Beauty:** Admire the intricate designs, carvings, and statues that adorn temples and pagodas.
- **Spiritual Serenity:** Experience the peaceful and meditative atmosphere of these sacred sites.
- **Cultural Insights:** Learn about the religious practices, rituals, and history associated with each temple and pagoda.

What to Expect:
- **Dress Modestly:** When visiting temples and pagodas, wear modest clothing that covers your shoulders and knees as a sign of respect.
- **Respectful Behavior:** Maintain a quiet and respectful demeanor, avoid loud conversations, and follow any posted rules or guidelines.
- **Offerings:** You may see locals making offerings of incense, flowers, and fruit. Visitors can also participate by making small offerings.

Visiting Tran Quoc Pagoda in Hanoi was a serene experience. The peaceful setting on West Lake and the beautiful gardens made it a perfect place for reflection. Thien Mu Pagoda in Hue offered stunning views of the Perfume River and a sense of tranquility. The scale and grandeur of Bai Dinh Pagoda in Ninh Binh were awe-inspiring, and the numerous Buddha statues added to its spiritual significance. The vibrant and intricate carvings at Jade Emperor Pagoda in Ho Chi Minh City provided a fascinating glimpse into Taoist traditions. One Pillar Pagoda in Hanoi was a unique architectural marvel that left a lasting impression.

Traditional Performances

Description: Traditional performances in Vietnam are a celebration of the country's artistic heritage, showcasing music, dance, theater, and puppetry. These performances provide a window into Vietnamese culture and history, allowing travelers to appreciate the artistic expressions and storytelling traditions that have been passed down through generations.

Examples of Traditional Performances:
1. **Water Puppetry (Hanoi):** A unique and ancient form of Vietnamese theater, water puppetry features wooden puppets performing on a water stage. The Thang Long Water Puppet Theatre in Hanoi is a popular venue for these enchanting performances.
2. **Ca Tru (Hanoi):** A traditional form of Vietnamese chamber music, Ca Tru involves singing, poetry, and instrumental accompaniment. Performances often take place in historic venues and offer an intimate cultural experience.
3. **Royal Court Music (Hue):** Known as Nha Nhac, this traditional music was performed at the royal court of the Nguyen Dynasty. The performances include music, dance, and elaborate costumes, providing a glimpse into the imperial culture of Hue.
4. **Hoi An Traditional Dance (Hoi An):** Experience traditional dance performances in the ancient town of Hoi An, where dancers in colorful costumes perform graceful and rhythmic movements to traditional music.
5. **Quan Ho Folk Songs (Bac Ninh):** A traditional form of folk singing from the Bac Ninh province, Quan Ho involves call-and-response duets performed by male and female singers. The songs often express themes of love and courtship.

Highlights:
- **Cultural Heritage:** Traditional performances offer a deeper understanding of Vietnam's artistic and cultural heritage.
- **Unique Art Forms:** Experience unique and ancient art forms, such as water puppetry and royal court music.
- **Captivating Storytelling**: Enjoy captivating storytelling through music, dance, and puppetry, with themes ranging from folklore to historical events.

What to Expect:
- **Theater Venues**: Performances often take place in traditional theaters, cultural centers, and historic venues. Arrive early to secure good seats.
- **Language Barrier**: While performances are typically in Vietnamese, the visual and musical aspects make them enjoyable and understandable for international audiences.
- **Respectful Audience**: Maintain a respectful and attentive demeanor during performances, and avoid using flash photography.

Watching a water puppetry performance at Thang Long Water Puppet Theatre in Hanoi was a magical experience. The skillful puppetry and traditional music created a captivating and unique show. Attending a Ca Tru performance in Hanoi provided an intimate and soulful experience, with the haunting melodies and poetic lyrics leaving a lasting impression. The royal court music and dance in Hue offered a glimpse into the grandeur of the imperial court, with elaborate costumes and graceful movements. Traditional dance performances in Hoi An added to the charm of the ancient town, and Quan Ho folk songs in Bac Ninh showcased the beauty of traditional Vietnamese singing.

Festivals and Celebrations

Description: Festivals and celebrations are an integral part of Vietnamese culture, with numerous events held throughout the year to mark important occasions, honor traditions, and bring communities together. Participating in these festivals provides a vibrant and joyous experience, allowing travelers to witness the country's rich cultural traditions and lively spirit.

Examples of Festivals and Celebrations:
1. **Tet Nguyen Dan (Lunar New Year):** Tet is the most important and widely celebrated festival in Vietnam, marking the Lunar New Year. Celebrations include family gatherings, special meals, fireworks, and traditional performances. Streets and homes are decorated with flowers and red banners to welcome the new year.
2. **Mid-Autumn Festival (Tet Trung Thu):** Celebrated on the 15th day of the eighth lunar month, the Mid-Autumn Festival is a time for family reunions and celebrations. Children enjoy lantern processions, mooncakes, and traditional lion dances.
3. **Hue Festival (Hue):** Held biennially in the historic city of Hue, this festival celebrates the cultural heritage of the Nguyen Dynasty with traditional music, dance, theater, and art exhibitions. The festival features events held at various historic sites in Hue.
4. **Hoi An Lantern Festival (Hoi An):** On the 14th day of each lunar month, Hoi An's ancient town is illuminated with colorful lanterns. The festival includes traditional music, dance, and cultural activities, creating a magical and enchanting atmosphere.
5. **Perfume Pagoda Festival (Hanoi):** A pilgrimage festival held at the Perfume Pagoda, attracting thousands of pilgrims who travel to the pagoda complex to pray for health and prosperity. The festival features boat trips, hiking, and traditional ceremonies.

Highlights:
- **Cultural Immersion:** Festivals provide an immersive experience of Vietnamese culture, traditions, and customs.
- **Joyous Celebrations**: Enjoy the festive atmosphere, vibrant decorations, and joyful activities that characterize these events.
- **Community Spirit**: Witness the strong sense of community and togetherness as locals come together to celebrate important occasions.

What to Expect:
- **Festive Atmosphere**: Expect lively celebrations with music, dance, food, and traditional rituals. Streets and public spaces are often beautifully decorated.
- **Crowds**: Festivals can attract large crowds, so be prepared for busy and bustling environments.
- **Traditional Attire:** During festivals, locals often wear traditional clothing,

such as ao dai (Vietnamese long dress) and other cultural attire.

Celebrating Tet in Hanoi was an unforgettable experience. The city was alive with festive decorations, fireworks, and family gatherings. The Mid-Autumn Festival in Hoi An was a magical event, with children carrying lanterns and enjoying mooncakes. The Hue Festival showcased the rich cultural heritage of the imperial city, with mesmerizing performances and art exhibitions. The Lantern Festival in Hoi An created a dreamy atmosphere with colorful lanterns lighting up the ancient town. Participating in the Perfume Pagoda Festival was a spiritual journey, with the scenic boat trip and hike to the pagoda adding to the significance of the pilgrimage.

Chapter 8: Shopping in Vietnam

Best Shopping Destinations

Vietnam offers a diverse and vibrant shopping scene, catering to all tastes and budgets. From bustling markets and traditional bazaars to modern shopping malls and charming artisan shops, there's something for every shopper. In this chapter, we'll explore the best shopping destinations in Vietnam, including markets and bazaars, shopping malls and boutiques, and artisan shops. Whether you're looking for unique souvenirs, fashion items, or handmade crafts, these shopping destinations will provide a memorable and enjoyable experience.

Markets and Bazaars

Description: Markets and bazaars are an integral part of Vietnamese culture and provide a lively and authentic shopping experience. These bustling hubs are perfect for finding fresh produce, local delicacies, clothing, accessories, and unique souvenirs. Visiting markets and bazaars allows you to immerse yourself in the local way of life and discover the vibrant atmosphere of Vietnamese commerce.

Examples of Markets and Bazaars:

1. **Ben Thanh Market (Ho Chi Minh City):** One of the oldest and most iconic markets in Vietnam, Ben Thanh Market offers a wide variety of goods, including clothing, souvenirs, handicrafts, and street food. It's a must-visit destination for any traveler to Ho Chi Minh City.
2. **Dong Xuan Market (Hanoi):** Located in the Old Quarter, Dong Xuan Market is a large indoor market selling everything from clothing and textiles to electronics and fresh produce. It's a great place to explore the local culture and find unique items.
3. **Hoi An Night Market (Hoi An):** This lively night market features colorful lanterns, handicrafts, jewelry, and delicious street food. It's an ideal spot for evening shopping and enjoying the vibrant atmosphere of Hoi An.
4. **Cai Rang Floating Market (Can Tho):** A unique market located on the Mekong River, Cai Rang Floating Market is a bustling hub of boats selling fresh produce, fruits, and local goods. Visiting this market provides a glimpse into the riverine lifestyle of the Mekong Delta.
5. **Cho Dam Market (Nha Trang):** A popular market in Nha Trang, Cho Dam Market offers a wide range of goods, including seafood, clothing, souvenirs, and household items. It's a great place to find bargains and experience the local culture.

Highlights:
- **Vibrant Atmosphere:** Experience the bustling and lively environment of Vietnamese markets and bazaars.
- **Diverse Products:** Find a wide variety of goods, from fresh produce and street food to clothing, accessories, and souvenirs.
- **Cultural Immersion:** Immerse yourself in the local way of life and interact with vendors and shoppers.

What to Expect:
- **Bargaining:** Bargaining is common in markets and bazaars. Be prepared to negotiate prices with vendors, and approach it with a friendly and respectful attitude.
- **Crowds:** Markets can be crowded, especially during peak hours. Be mindful of your belongings and enjoy the lively atmosphere.
- **Cash Transactions:** Most vendors prefer cash, so bring enough local currency (Vietnamese Dong) for your purchases.

Exploring Ben Thanh Market in Ho Chi Minh City was an exciting experience. The market's diverse offerings and vibrant atmosphere made it a great place to find souvenirs and sample local street food. Dong Xuan Market in Hanoi provided a fascinating glimpse into the city's commercial life, with its wide range of products and bustling environment. The colorful lanterns and lively ambiance of Hoi An Night Market made evening shopping a memorable experience. Visiting Cai Rang Floating Market in the Mekong Delta was a unique adventure, with boats filled with fresh produce and local goods creating a picturesque scene.

Shopping Malls and Boutiques

Description: Vietnam's shopping malls and boutiques offer a modern and stylish shopping experience, with a wide range of international and local brands, fashion items, electronics, and luxury goods. These destinations provide a comfortable and convenient shopping environment, often featuring air-conditioned spaces, entertainment options, and dining areas.

Examples of Shopping Malls and Boutiques:
1. **Vincom Center (Ho Chi Minh City):** A large and modern shopping mall located in District 1, Vincom Center features a wide range of international and local brands, fashion boutiques, electronics stores, and dining options.
2. **Trang Tien Plaza (Hanoi):** An upscale shopping mall situated near Hoan Kiem Lake, Trang Tien Plaza offers luxury brands, designer boutiques, and a selection of high-end goods in an elegant setting.
3. **Lotte Center (Hanoi):** A towering shopping and entertainment complex with a variety of shops, including fashion, electronics, and cosmetics. The observation deck offers stunning views of Hanoi's skyline.
4. **Parkson Saigon Tourist Plaza (Ho Chi Minh City):** A well-known department store featuring a wide range of fashion, beauty, and lifestyle products from international and local brands.

5. **Diamond Plaza (Ho Chi Minh City)**: A modern shopping mall offering fashion, electronics, homeware, and dining options. The mall also includes entertainment facilities such as a cinema and bowling alley.

Highlights:
- **Modern Shopping Experience:** Enjoy a comfortable and stylish shopping environment with a wide range of products and services.
- **International and Local Brands**: Find popular international brands as well as unique local boutiques offering fashion, beauty, and lifestyle products.
- **Entertainment and Dining:** Many shopping malls feature entertainment options, such as cinemas and arcades, as well as a variety of dining choices.

What to Expect:
- **Fixed Prices:** Unlike markets and bazaars, prices in shopping malls and boutiques are usually fixed, and bargaining is not common.
- **Air-Conditioned Comfort**: Shopping malls provide a comfortable and air-conditioned environment, making them a great option for escaping the heat.

- **Payment Options**: Most stores accept credit cards, but it's always good to carry some cash for smaller purchases.

Shopping at Vincom Center in Ho Chi Minh City was a pleasant experience, with its wide range of stores and modern facilities. Trang Tien Plaza in Hanoi offered a luxurious shopping experience with high-end brands and elegant surroundings. The observation deck at Lotte Center provided stunning views of Hanoi, adding to the enjoyment of the shopping trip. Parkson Saigon Tourist Plaza and Diamond Plaza in Ho Chi Minh City featured a diverse selection of fashion and lifestyle products, as well as convenient dining options.

Artisan Shops

Description: Artisan shops in Vietnam offer unique and handmade crafts, including textiles, ceramics, lacquerware, jewelry, and traditional art. These shops provide an opportunity to support local artisans and bring home one-of-a-kind souvenirs that reflect Vietnam's rich cultural heritage and craftsmanship.

Examples of Artisan Shops:
1. **Craft Link (Hanoi):** A non-profit organization that supports ethnic minority artisans, Craft Link offers a wide range of handmade products, including textiles, clothing, home decor, and traditional crafts.
2. **Rehahn Gallery (Hoi An):** A gallery and shop featuring the photography and art of Réhahn, as well as unique handcrafted items such as jewelry, textiles, and ceramics. The gallery also supports local artisans and ethnic minority communities.
3. **Tan My Design (Hanoi):** A renowned shop offering high-quality silk products, including clothing, accessories, and home decor. Tan My Design combines traditional craftsmanship with modern design.
4. **Saigon Kitsch (Ho Chi Minh City):** A quirky shop offering a variety of unique and creative souvenirs, including art prints, home decor, and accessories that showcase contemporary Vietnamese culture.
5. **Sapa O'Chau (Sapa):** An artisan shop and social enterprise supporting ethnic minority communities in Sapa. The shop offers handmade textiles, clothing, and crafts, with proceeds going to community development projects.

Highlights:
- **Unique Souvenirs:** Discover one-of-a-kind handmade products that reflect Vietnam's cultural heritage and craftsmanship.
- **Supporting Local Artisans:** Purchase from artisan shops to support local craftsmen and their communities.
- **High-Quality Craftsmanship**: Find high-quality and beautifully crafted items, including textiles, ceramics, jewelry, and traditional art.

What to Expect:
- **Authenticity**: Artisan shops offer authentic and handmade products that are often unique to the region.
- **Fair Prices**: Prices in artisan shops may be higher than in markets, reflecting the quality and craftsmanship of the products. Bargaining is usually not practiced.

- **Cultural Significance**: Many artisan products have cultural and historical significance, making them meaningful souvenirs.

Visiting Craft Link in Hanoi was a rewarding experience, as I found beautifully crafted textiles and home decor items while supporting local artisans. Rehahn Gallery in Hoi An offered stunning photography and unique handcrafted items that captured the essence of Vietnamese culture. Shopping at Tan My Design provided high-quality silk products with a blend of traditional and modern designs. Saigon Kitsch in Ho Chi Minh City was a fun and creative shop with unique souvenirs that reflected contemporary Vietnamese culture. Sapa O'Chau in Sapa offered beautiful handmade textiles and crafts while contributing to community development projects.

What to Buy: Exploring Vietnam's vibrant markets, boutiques, and artisan shops offers a fantastic opportunity to bring home unique and memorable items. From traditional handicrafts to local products, there's a wide variety of goods to choose from. In this section, we'll cover the best souvenirs and handicrafts, local products, and provide shopping tips and bargaining advice to help you make the most of your shopping experience in Vietnam.

Souvenirs and Handicrafts

Description: Vietnam is known for its rich cultural heritage and skilled craftsmanship, making it an excellent destination for finding unique and beautiful souvenirs and handicrafts. These items not only serve as mementos of your trip but also reflect the country's artistic traditions and cultural diversity.

Examples of Souvenirs and Handicrafts:

1. **Silk Products**: Vietnam is famous for its high-quality silk, and you can find a variety of silk products, including scarves, clothing, accessories, and embroidered items. Hoi An is a particularly well-known destination for silk shopping.
2. **Lacquerware**: Lacquerware is a traditional Vietnamese craft involving layers of lacquer to create beautiful and durable items. Look for lacquerware boxes, trays, vases, and wall art with intricate designs.
3. **Ceramics**: Handcrafted ceramics, such as bowls, plates, and vases, make wonderful souvenirs. Bat Trang, a village near Hanoi, is renowned for its pottery and ceramics.
4. **Wooden Artifacts:** Wooden carvings and sculptures, including figurines, masks, and traditional art pieces, are popular souvenirs that showcase the skill of Vietnamese woodworkers.
5. **Ao Dai:** The ao dai is the traditional Vietnamese long dress, and it makes a beautiful and elegant souvenir. You can find ready-made ao dai or have one custom-tailored in cities like Hanoi and Ho Chi Minh City.

Highlights:

- **Unique and Beautiful:** Souvenirs and handicrafts in Vietnam are often unique, beautifully crafted, and reflect the country's artistic heritage.
- **Cultural Significance:** Many items have cultural and historical significance, making them meaningful mementos of your trip.

- **Skilled Craftsmanship**: Vietnamese artisans are known for their skill and attention to detail, resulting in high-quality products.

Shopping for silk products in Hoi An was a delightful experience. The variety of colors and designs, along with the high quality of the silk, made it easy to find beautiful scarves and clothing. Exploring lacquerware shops in Hanoi revealed stunningly detailed pieces, perfect for gifts and home decor. Visiting Bat Trang village allowed me to see the pottery-making process firsthand and purchase unique ceramic items. Finding a custom-tailored ao dai in Ho Chi Minh City provided a special and elegant souvenir that I'll cherish forever.

Local Products

Description: Vietnam is also known for its diverse range of local products, including food items, beverages, and traditional remedies. These products make excellent souvenirs and provide a taste of Vietnam's culinary and wellness traditions.

Examples of Local Products:
1. **Coffee**: Vietnamese coffee is famous for its rich and bold flavor. Bring home some coffee beans or ground coffee to enjoy the distinctive taste of Vietnamese coffee. Popular types include robusta and arabica.
2. **Tea**: Vietnam produces a variety of high-quality teas, including green tea, jasmine tea, and lotus tea. These aromatic teas make wonderful gifts and can be found in local markets and specialty shops.
3. **Fish Sauce**: A staple in Vietnamese cuisine, fish sauce is a versatile and flavorful condiment. Look for high-quality fish sauce from Phu Quoc Island, known for its traditional production methods.
4. **Spices and Herbs:** Vietnamese cuisine uses a variety of spices and herbs, such as star anise, cinnamon, and lemongrass. These can be found in local markets and make great additions to your kitchen back home.
5. **Traditional Medicine:** Herbal remedies and traditional medicine products are widely available in Vietnam. These include herbal teas, balms, and natural supplements, often used for wellness and healing.

Highlights:
- **Culinary Delights:** Bring home the flavors of Vietnam with local food and beverage products.
- **High-Quality**: Local products are often produced using traditional methods and high-quality ingredients.
- **Useful and Enjoyable:** These items are not only enjoyable souvenirs but also practical additions to your daily life.

Bringing home Vietnamese coffee allowed me to savor the rich and bold flavors of the country's coffee culture. The aromatic teas, especially lotus and jasmine tea, made perfect gifts for friends and family. High-quality fish sauce from Phu Quoc Island added a delicious Vietnamese touch to my cooking. The spices and herbs I found in local markets brought the authentic flavors of Vietnamese cuisine to my kitchen. Exploring traditional medicine shops provided interesting insights into local wellness practices and remedies.

Shopping Tips and Bargaining

Description: Shopping in Vietnam can be an enjoyable and rewarding experience, especially if you know how to navigate the markets and make the most of your shopping trips. Here are some tips and advice on bargaining to help you get the best deals and have a positive shopping experience.

Shopping Tips:
- **Research and Plan:** Before you go shopping, research the best places to find the items you're looking for and plan your visit accordingly. This will help you save time and find the best deals.
- **Inspect the Quality**: Take your time to inspect the quality of the items you're interested in. Check for any defects or damage, and ensure the craftsmanship meets your expectations.
- **Carry Cash**: While many shops and malls accept credit cards, markets and smaller vendors often prefer cash. Carry enough local currency (Vietnamese Dong) to make your purchases.
- **Be Polite**: Approach your shopping experience with a friendly and respectful attitude. Politeness goes a long way in building rapport with vendors and getting better deals.

Bargaining Tips:
- **Start with a Smile:** Begin the bargaining process with a smile and a friendly demeanor. This sets a positive tone for the negotiation.
- **Know the Market Price**: Have a general idea of the market price for the items you're interested in. This will give you a benchmark to start your negotiations.
- **Make a Counteroffer**: If the initial price quoted by the vendor is too high, make a reasonable counteroffer. Aim for a price that's about 30-50% lower than the initial offer.
- **Be Patient**: Bargaining can take time, so be patient and don't rush the process. Vendors may be more willing to lower the price if you take your time and show genuine interest.
- **Be Willing to Walk Away**: If the vendor is not willing to meet your price, be prepared to walk away. Sometimes, this can prompt the vendor to lower the price. If not, you can always find similar items elsewhere.

Bargaining at Ben Thanh Market in Ho Chi Minh City was a fun and rewarding experience. Starting with a smile and being polite helped build rapport with vendors, and I was able to negotiate good deals on souvenirs. Researching market prices and inspecting the quality of items at Dong Xuan Market in Hanoi ensured that I made informed purchases. Carrying cash and being patient during the bargaining process at Hoi An Night Market led to successful negotiations and enjoyable shopping experiences.

Chapter 9: Culture and Etiquette

Understanding Vietnamese Culture

Vietnam is a country with a rich cultural heritage and deep-rooted traditions. Understanding Vietnamese culture and social etiquette can greatly enhance your travel experience, allowing you to connect more meaningfully with the local people and show respect for their customs. In this chapter, we'll explore key cultural norms and social etiquette to help you navigate Vietnamese society with ease and respect.

Key Cultural Norms and Social Etiquette

Description: Vietnamese culture is influenced by Confucianism, Buddhism, and Taoism, along with centuries of history and diverse ethnic traditions. Social interactions in Vietnam are guided by a set of cultural norms and etiquette that emphasize respect, harmony, and consideration for others. Here are some key aspects to keep in mind:

1. **Respect for Elders:** Elders hold a special place in Vietnamese society and are highly respected. When interacting with older individuals, show deference and use respectful language. It's customary to allow elders to speak first, offer them seats, and serve them food and drinks before serving yourself.

2. **Polite Greetings**: Greetings in Vietnam are often accompanied by a slight bow or nod. The traditional greeting involves clasping your hands together in front of you, similar to a prayer position, and bowing slightly. Handshakes are also common, especially in more formal settings, but they may be softer than in Western cultures.

3. **Addressing People**: Titles and proper forms of address are important in Vietnam. Use "Anh" (older brother) or "Chi" (older sister) for addressing individuals slightly older than you. "Co" (aunt) or "Chu" (uncle) can be used for those significantly older. For younger people, use "Em" (younger sibling). Addressing people by their titles followed by their first name is a sign of respect.

4. **Modesty and Humility:** Modesty and humility are valued traits in Vietnamese culture. Avoid boasting or showing off, and be humble in your accomplishments. When complimented, it's common to respond with modesty rather than accepting the praise outright.

5. **Gift-Giving Etiquette:** Giving and receiving gifts is a common practice in Vietnam, especially during special occasions and visits. When offering a gift, present it with both hands as a sign of respect. Gifts are often not opened in front of the giver. Avoid giving sharp objects, black or white items, as these are associated with funerals.

6. **Dining Etiquette**: During meals, it's customary to wait for the eldest person to start eating before you begin. Use chopsticks properly and avoid sticking them upright in a bowl of rice, as this resembles incense sticks used in funerals. Sharing dishes and using communal chopsticks for serving is common practice.

7. **Dress Code**: Modesty in dress is appreciated, especially when visiting religious

sites such as temples and pagodas. Avoid wearing revealing or inappropriate clothing. Remove your shoes before entering someone's home or a sacred place.

8. **Personal Space and Physical Contact**: Vietnamese people may have different perceptions of personal space compared to Western cultures. Touching someone's head is considered disrespectful, as the head is considered the most sacred part of the body. Physical displays of affection, such as hugging and kissing, are less common in public.

Highlights:
- **Respectful Interactions:** Emphasize respect, humility, and consideration in your interactions with others.
- **Cultural Sensitivity**: Show awareness and sensitivity to local customs and traditions.
- **Meaningful Connections**: Understanding and following cultural norms can lead to more meaningful and positive interactions with the local people.

What to Expect:
- **Warm Hospitality**: Vietnamese people are known for their warm hospitality and friendliness. Showing respect and understanding of their culture will enhance your experience.
- **Traditional Values**: Many aspects of Vietnamese culture are deeply rooted in tradition and history, influencing daily life and social interactions.
- **Cultural Diversity**: Vietnam is home to diverse ethnic groups, each with its own customs and traditions. Be open to learning and appreciating these differences.

During my travels in Vietnam, observing respect for elders and addressing people with the appropriate titles helped build positive and respectful relationships. Participating in traditional greetings and showing modesty in conversations fostered a sense of connection with the local people. Gift-giving during special occasions was a meaningful practice, and understanding dining etiquette made shared meals more enjoyable. Dressing modestly when visiting temples and pagodas showed respect for the sacred spaces and local customs. Overall, embracing Vietnamese cultural norms and social etiquette enriched my travel experience and deepened my appreciation for the country's rich cultural heritage.

Language Tips

Learning a few common phrases and basic Vietnamese can greatly enhance your travel experience in Vietnam. It shows respect for the local culture, helps you navigate daily interactions, and can create more meaningful connections with the local people. In this section, we'll cover common phrases and greetings, as well as basic Vietnamese for travelers.

Common Phrases and Greetings

Description: Using common phrases and greetings in Vietnamese can help you break the ice and show politeness in social interactions. Here are some essential phrases to get you started:

Greetings:
- Hello / Hi: Xin chào (sin chow)
- Good morning: Chào buổi sáng (chow bwoo-ee sahng)
- Good afternoon: Chào buổi chiều (chow bwoo-ee chee-oh)
- Good evening: Chào buổi tối (chow bwoo-ee toy)
- Goodbye: Tạm biệt (tahm bee-eht)

Polite Expressions:
- Please: Làm ơn (lahm uhn)
- Thank you: Cảm ơn (gahm uhn)
- You're welcome: Không có gì (kohng kaw zee)
- Excuse me / Sorry: Xin lỗi (sin loy)
- Yes: Vâng / Dạ (vuhng / yah)
- No: Không (kohng)

Basic Conversations:
- How are you?: Bạn khỏe không? (bahn kweh kohng)
- I'm fine, thank you: Tôi khỏe, cảm ơn (toy kweh, gahm uhn)
- What is your name?: Bạn tên là gì? (bahn tehn lah zee)
- My name is [Your Name]: Tên tôi là [Your Name] (tehn toy lah [Your Name])
- Nice to meet you: Rất vui được gặp bạn (zuht voo-ee duhrk gahp bahn)

Numbers:
- One: Một (moht)
- Two: Hai (hi)
- Three: Ba (bah)
- Four: Bốn (bohn)
- Five: Năm (nahm)
- Six: Sáu (sow)
- Seven: Bảy (bye)
- Eight: Tám (tahm)
- Nine: Chín (cheen)
- Ten: Mười (moo-ee)

Highlights:
- **Politeness and Respect**: Using greetings and polite expressions shows respect and consideration for the local culture.
- **Positive Interactions**: Simple phrases can help create positive interactions and make you feel more confident in social situations.
- **Easy to Learn**: These common phrases are easy to learn and can be used in various contexts.

Using basic greetings like "Xin chào" and "Cảm ơn" during my travels in Vietnam was always met with warm smiles and appreciation from locals. It made interactions more enjoyable and showed respect for the local culture. Simple phrases like "Làm ơn" and "Xin lỗi" helped navigate daily interactions with politeness and ease.

Basic Vietnamese for Travelers

Description: Learning a few more basic Vietnamese phrases can help you navigate common travel situations, such as ordering food, asking for directions, and shopping. Here are some useful phrases for travelers:

Dining and Food:
- Menu: Thực đơn (thook duhn)
- I would like to order: Tôi muốn gọi món (toy mwun goy mawn)
- What do you recommend?: Bạn giới thiệu món gì? (bahn zoy thee-u mawn zee)
- Delicious: Ngon (ngawn)
- Check, please: Tính tiền, làm ơn (tinh tee-ehn, lahm uhn)

Asking for Directions:
- Where is [place]?: [Place] ở đâu? ([Place] uh dow?)
- How do I get to [place]?: Làm sao tôi đến được [place]? (lahm sow toy dein duhrk [place]?)
- Left: Trái (chay)
- Right: Phải (fie)
- Straight ahead: Thẳng (tahng)

Shopping:
- How much is this?: Cái này bao nhiêu tiền? (gai nigh bow nyeu tee-ehn)
- Expensive: Đắt (daht)
- Cheap: Rẻ (zeh)
- Can you lower the price?: Bạn có thể giảm giá không? (bahn kaw teh yahm zah kohng)
- I'll buy it: Tôi mua cái này (toy moo-ah gai nigh)

Accommodation:
- Hotel: Khách sạn (khahk sahn)
- Room: Phòng (fong)
- Reservation: Đặt phòng (daht fong)
- Check-in: Nhận phòng (nyun fong)
- Check-out: Trả phòng (chah fong)

Emergency:
- Help!: Cứu! (ku)
- I need a doctor: Tôi cần bác sĩ (toy kuhn bahk see)
- Call the police: Gọi cảnh sát (goy kahng saht)

Highlights:
- Practical Phrases: These phrases are practical and useful for navigating common travel situations.
- Increased Confidence: Knowing basic Vietnamese can boost your confidence and make your travels smoother.
- Positive Impressions: Locals appreciate the effort to speak their language, leading to positive and memorable interactions.

Ordering food with phrases like "Tôi muốn gọi món" and expressing appreciation with "Ngon" made dining experiences more enjoyable and helped connect with local vendors. Asking for directions with "Làm sao tôi đến được [place]?" and understanding basic directional terms like "Trái" and "Phải" made navigating unfamiliar places easier. Shopping with phrases like "Cái này bao nhiêu tiền?" and bargaining with "Bạn có thể giảm giá không?" led to successful and pleasant shopping experiences. Knowing emergency phrases provided a sense of security and preparedness during my travels.

Chapter 10: Health and Safety

Staying Healthy

Traveling to Vietnam is an exciting adventure, but it's important to prioritize your health and safety to ensure a smooth and enjoyable trip. In this chapter, we'll cover recommended vaccinations, medical facilities and pharmacies, and provide health and safety tips to help you stay healthy during your travels.

Recommended Vaccinations

Description: Before traveling to Vietnam, it's important to ensure that you are up-to-date on routine vaccinations and consider additional vaccinations that may be recommended based on your travel itinerary and activities. Here are some key vaccinations to consider:

Routine Vaccinations:
- Measles, Mumps, Rubella (MMR): Ensure you have received the MMR vaccine, as outbreaks can still occur in some regions.
- **Diphtheria, Tetanus, Pertussis (DTaP):** Stay up-to-date on your DTaP vaccination to protect against these common infections.
- **Varicella (Chickenpox)**: Ensure you are vaccinated against chickenpox, especially if you have not had the disease.

Travel-Specific Vaccinations:
- **Hepatitis A:** Recommended for all travelers, as the virus can be transmitted through contaminated food and water.
- **Hepatitis B:** Recommended for travelers who may have exposure to blood or body fluids, including through medical procedures or sexual contact.
- **Typhoid**: Recommended for travelers, especially if you plan to visit rural areas or consume food and drinks from street vendors.
- **Japanese Encephalitis**: Recommended for travelers spending extended periods in rural areas or participating in outdoor activities, especially during the transmission season.
- **Rabies**: Considered for travelers who may have close contact with animals or are at higher risk of animal bites.
- **Malaria**: Depending on your travel itinerary, you may need to take malaria prophylaxis. Consult with a healthcare provider for recommendations based on specific regions.

Highlights:
- **Preventive Measures**: Vaccinations are a key preventive measure to protect your health while traveling.
- **Consult a Healthcare Provider**: It's important to consult with a healthcare provider or travel medicine specialist to receive personalized recommendations based on your health status and travel plans.

Before my trip to Vietnam, I consulted with a travel medicine specialist who recommended the Hepatitis A and Typhoid vaccines based on my travel itinerary. The consultation provided valuable information on preventive measures and ensured I was well-prepared for my journey.

Medical Facilities and Pharmacies

Description: Vietnam has a range of medical facilities and pharmacies that cater to both locals and travelers. Understanding the availability and quality of healthcare services can help you feel more secure during your trip.

Examples of Medical Facilities:
1. **Hanoi French Hospital (Hanoi):** A reputable international hospital providing comprehensive medical services, including emergency care, consultations, and specialized treatments.
2. **FV Hospital (Ho Chi Minh City):** An internationally accredited hospital offering a wide range of medical services, including inpatient and outpatient care, diagnostics, and specialized treatments.
3. **Vinmec International Hospital (Da Nang, Hanoi, Ho Chi Minh City):** A network of modern hospitals providing high-quality healthcare services, including general medicine, surgery, and emergency care.
4. **Family Medical Practice (Hanoi, Ho Chi Minh City, Da Nang):** A medical clinic chain offering healthcare services for expatriates and travelers, including general practice, emergency care, and specialized consultations.

Pharmacies:
- **Local Pharmacies**: Pharmacies are widely available throughout Vietnam, especially in urban areas. Look for reputable pharmacies with licensed pharmacists to ensure the quality of medications.
- **Hospital Pharmacies**: Many hospitals have in-house pharmacies where you can fill prescriptions and obtain medications recommended by healthcare providers.

Highlights:
- **Quality Healthcare:** Vietnam has reputable international hospitals and medical clinics that provide high-quality healthcare services.
- **Accessibility**: Medical facilities and pharmacies are easily accessible, especially in major cities and tourist areas.
- **English-Speaking Staff:** Many international hospitals and clinics have English-speaking staff to assist foreign travelers.

During my travels in Vietnam, I visited a Family Medical Practice clinic in Ho Chi Minh City for a routine check-up. The staff was professional and courteous, and the English-speaking doctor provided clear and comprehensive care. When I needed to purchase over-the-counter medication, the local pharmacy staff in Hanoi was helpful and provided the necessary guidance.

Health and Safety Tips

Description: Taking proactive measures to stay healthy and safe during your travels can help ensure a smooth and enjoyable experience. Here are some essential health and safety tips for traveling in Vietnam:

1. **Food and Water Safety:**

- Drink bottled or purified water and avoid tap water and ice made from tap water.
- Choose freshly cooked food and avoid raw or undercooked dishes, especially from street vendors.
- Wash your hands frequently with soap and water or use hand sanitizer.

2. **Mosquito Protection:**
   - Use insect repellent containing DEET or picaridin to protect against mosquito bites.
   - Wear long-sleeved clothing and pants, especially during dawn and dusk when mosquitoes are most active.
   - Sleep under mosquito nets or use mosquito screens on windows and doors.

3. **Sun Protection:**
   - Apply sunscreen with a high SPF to protect against UV rays, especially during outdoor activities.
   - Wear a wide-brimmed hat and sunglasses to shield yourself from the sun.

4. **Personal Safety:**
   - Be cautious with your belongings and avoid displaying valuable items in public.
   - Use reputable transportation services and avoid unlicensed taxis or motorbikes.
   - Stay aware of your surroundings and avoid walking alone in unfamiliar or isolated areas at night.

5. **Travel Insurance:**
   - Purchase comprehensive travel insurance that covers medical emergencies, trip cancellations, and theft or loss of belongings.
   - Carry a copy of your insurance policy and emergency contact numbers.

Highlights:
- **Proactive Measures:** Taking proactive health and safety measures can prevent common travel-related illnesses and incidents.
- **Peace of Mind**: Being prepared with travel insurance and knowledge of local healthcare services provides peace of mind.
- **Enjoyable Travel:** Staying healthy and safe allows you to fully enjoy your travel experiences without interruptions.

Following food and water safety guidelines helped me avoid digestive issues during my travels in Vietnam. Using mosquito repellent and wearing long-sleeved clothing provided effective protection against mosquito bites, especially in rural areas. Staying aware of my surroundings and using reputable transportation services ensured my personal safety and allowed me to explore the country with confidence. Having travel insurance provided reassurance in case of unexpected emergencies.

Staying Safe

While Vietnam is generally considered a safe destination for travelers, taking some basic precautions can ensure your safety and enhance your travel experience. In this section, we'll cover general safety tips to help you stay safe and secure during your journey.

General Safety Tips

Description: Following general safety tips can help you avoid common risks and ensure a smooth and enjoyable trip. Here are some key safety tips to keep in mind:

1. **Be Aware of Your Surroundings:** Stay vigilant and aware of your surroundings, especially in crowded areas, tourist attractions, and public transportation. Keep an eye on your belongings and be mindful of potential pickpockets.
2. **Keep Valuables Secure:** Avoid displaying valuable items, such as jewelry, expensive gadgets, and large amounts of cash, in public. Use a money belt or a secure bag to keep your belongings safe.
3. **Use Reputable Transportation**: Use reputable and licensed transportation services, such as registered taxis, ride-sharing apps (e.g., Grab), and hotel-arranged transport. Avoid using unlicensed taxis or accepting rides from strangers.
4. **Stay in Well-Lit Areas**: Stick to well-lit and populated areas, especially at night. Avoid walking alone in unfamiliar or isolated areas, and use transportation to get back to your accommodation safely.
5. **Avoid Scams**: Be cautious of common scams targeting tourists, such as overcharging, fake goods, and unsolicited offers. Research and be aware of common scams in the area you are visiting, and trust your instincts if something feels off.
6. **Keep Important Documents Safe**: Make copies of important documents, such as your passport, visa, and travel insurance. Keep the originals in a secure place, such as a hotel safe, and carry the copies with you.
7. **Stay Connected**: Keep your phone charged and ensure you have access to local emergency numbers, your accommodation's contact information, and the contact details of your country's embassy or consulate.
8. **Respect Local Laws and Customs**: Familiarize yourself with local laws and customs to avoid any unintentional offenses. Behave respectfully and follow cultural norms, especially when visiting religious sites and interacting with locals.
9. **Travel Insurance**: Purchase comprehensive travel insurance that covers medical emergencies, trip cancellations, theft, and loss of belongings. Ensure you have a copy of your insurance policy and emergency contact numbers.

Highlights:

- **Proactive Measures:** Taking proactive safety measures can help prevent common risks and ensure a worry-free trip.
- **Peace of Mind**: Being prepared and aware of your surroundings provides peace of mind and allows you to enjoy your travels with confidence.
- **Respectful Behavior**: Respecting local laws, customs, and cultural norms enhances your travel experience and fosters positive interactions with locals.

Staying vigilant and aware of my surroundings in crowded areas, such as markets and tourist attractions, helped me avoid potential pickpocketing incidents. Using reputable transportation services, like Grab and hotel-arranged taxis, ensured safe and reliable travel between destinations. Keeping important documents secure and carrying copies provided peace of mind in case of any unexpected situations. Being respectful of local laws and customs, especially when visiting temples and interacting with locals, fostered positive experiences and meaningful connections during my travels.

Common Scams and How to Avoid Them

When traveling to Vietnam, being aware of common scams and knowing how to avoid them can help ensure a safe and enjoyable trip. Scammers often target tourists, so it's important to stay vigilant and take precautions. In this section, we'll cover some common scams and provide tips on how to avoid them.

Description: Scammers use various tactics to deceive travelers and take advantage of their unfamiliarity with the local environment. Here are some common scams you may encounter and tips on how to avoid them:

1. **Taxi Scams:**
   - **Description**: Unlicensed or dishonest taxi drivers may overcharge you by taking longer routes, using rigged meters, or quoting inflated fares.
   - **How to Avoid:** Use reputable and licensed taxi companies, such as Mai Linh and Vinasun. Alternatively, use ride-sharing apps like Grab, which provide fare estimates and track your route. Confirm the fare before starting the journey and insist on using the meter.
2. **Fake Tour Guides:**
   - **Description**: Scammers posing as tour guides may offer to show you around, only to overcharge you or take you to places where they receive kickbacks from vendors.
   - **How to Avoid**: Book tours through reputable travel agencies or your accommodation. Check reviews and recommendations online before hiring a guide.
3. **Fake Goods:**
   - **Description**: Some markets and shops sell counterfeit or low-quality goods, passing them off as genuine products.
   - **How to Avoid**: Be cautious when purchasing branded items and luxury goods. Shop at reputable stores and verify the authenticity of the products. If the deal seems too good to be true, it probably is.
4. **Pickpocketing:**
   - **Description:** Pickpockets often target tourists in crowded areas, markets, and public transportation.
   - **How to Avoid**: Keep your belongings secure and avoid displaying valuable items. Use a money belt or a secure bag with zippers. Stay vigilant in crowded places and be cautious of distractions.
5. **Money Exchange Scams:**
   - **Description:** Some money exchange services may offer unfavorable rates or shortchange you during the transaction.
   - **How to Avoid:** Exchange money at reputable banks, exchange offices, or ATMs. Count your money carefully before leaving the counter and be aware of the current exchange rate.
6. **Overpriced Souvenirs:**

- **Description:** Some vendors may charge tourists significantly higher prices for souvenirs and goods.
- **How to Avoid:** Bargain politely and be prepared to walk away if the price is too high. Research typical prices for common souvenirs to have a baseline for negotiations.

7. **Motorbike Rental Scams:**
   - **Description**: Some motorbike rental shops may rent out poorly maintained bikes or charge exorbitant fees for minor damages.
   - **How to Avoid:** Rent motorbikes from reputable shops with good reviews. Inspect the bike thoroughly before renting and take photos of any existing damage. Clarify the rental terms and fees in advance.

Highlights:
- **Proactive Measures:** Taking proactive safety measures can help prevent common risks and ensure a worry-free trip.
- **Peace of Mind**: Being prepared and aware of your surroundings provides peace of mind and allows you to enjoy your travels with confidence.
- **Respectful Behavior:** Respecting local laws, customs, and cultural norms enhances your travel experience and fosters positive interactions with locals.

Using ride-sharing apps like Grab provided transparent fares and safe transportation during my travels. Booking tours through reputable agencies ensured knowledgeable and trustworthy guides. Shopping at reputable stores and verifying product authenticity helped avoid counterfeit goods. Keeping my belongings secure and staying vigilant in crowded areas prevented pickpocketing incidents. Exchanging money at banks and counting it carefully ensured fair transactions.

Emergency Contacts and Services

Knowing emergency contacts and services in Vietnam can provide peace of mind and ensure you are prepared for any unexpected situations. Here are some key emergency contacts and services to keep in mind:

Emergency Contacts:
- Police: 113
- Fire Department: 114
- Ambulance/Medical Emergency: 115

Key Services:
1. **Embassies and Consulates:**
   - **Description:** Your country's embassy or consulate can provide assistance in case of emergencies, such as lost passports, legal issues, or medical emergencies.
   - Contact Information: Keep a list of contact details for your country's embassy or consulate in Vietnam.
2. **Travel Insurance Provider:**
   - **Description:** In case of medical emergencies or other travel-related issues, contact your travel insurance provider for assistance and claims.
   - **Contact Information**: Carry a copy of your travel insurance policy and emergency contact numbers.
3. **Medical Facilities:**

- **Description**: Familiarize yourself with nearby hospitals and clinics that provide medical services for travelers.
- **Key Facilities**: Hanoi French Hospital (Hanoi), FV Hospital (Ho Chi Minh City), Vinmec International Hospital (various locations).

Highlights:

- **Preparedness:** Having emergency contact information readily available ensures you are prepared for any unexpected situations.
- **Peace of Mind**: Knowing how to reach emergency services and where to seek assistance provides peace of mind during your travels.
- **Quick Response**: Access to emergency contacts and services ensures a quick response in case of emergencies, minimizing potential risks.

Carrying a list of emergency contacts and embassy details provided reassurance during my travels in Vietnam. Knowing the contact information for nearby medical facilities and having travel insurance ensured I was prepared for any medical emergencies. Familiarizing myself with the local emergency numbers and services helped me feel more secure and confident while exploring the country.

Chapter 11: Practical Information

Money Matters

Managing your finances while traveling in Vietnam is essential for a smooth and stress-free experience. Understanding the local currency, banking options, and tipping etiquette will help you navigate financial transactions with ease. In this chapter, we'll cover currency and exchange, banking and ATMs, and tipping etiquette.

Currency and Exchange

Description: Vietnam's official currency is the Vietnamese Dong (VND). Understanding how to exchange and manage your money is crucial for handling daily expenses and transactions.

Currency Information:
- Currency Symbol: ₫
- Common Denominations: Banknotes come in various denominations, including 1,000, 2,000, 5,000, 10,000, 20,000, 50,000, 100,000, 200,000, and 500,000 VND. Coins are less commonly used.

Currency Exchange:
- **Exchange Locations**: You can exchange foreign currency at banks, exchange offices, hotels, and airports. Banks and official exchange offices typically offer better rates than hotels and airports.
- **Popular Currencies**: US Dollars (USD), Euros (EUR), and other major currencies are widely accepted for exchange.
- **Exchange Rates**: Be aware of the current exchange rates and compare rates at different locations to get the best deal.

Tips for Currency Exchange:
- **Avoid Black Market**: Exchange money at reputable banks or exchange offices to avoid scams and counterfeit currency.
- **Small Denominations**: Carry small denominations of VND for everyday transactions, as it may be difficult to get change for larger bills.
- **Receipt**: Always ask for a receipt when exchanging money and count your cash before leaving the counter.

Exchanging money at a reputable bank in Hanoi provided better rates and a secure transaction. Carrying small denominations of VND made it easier to pay for street food, transportation, and small purchases. Comparing exchange rates at different locations ensured I received the best value for my foreign currency.

Banking and ATMs

Description: Banking services and ATMs are widely available throughout Vietnam, making it convenient to withdraw cash and manage your finances while traveling.

Banking Services:

- **Local Banks:** Major local banks include Vietcombank, VietinBank, and BIDV, offering a range of banking services for both locals and tourists.
- **International Banks:** Some international banks, such as HSBC and ANZ, have branches in major cities, providing services for expatriates and travelers.

ATMs:

- **Availability:** ATMs are widely available in cities, towns, and tourist areas, allowing you to withdraw cash in VND.
- **Withdrawal Limits:** Be aware of the withdrawal limits, which may vary by bank and ATM. Some ATMs may have lower limits for foreign cards.
- **Fees**: Check with your home bank about international ATM fees and currency conversion fees. Some banks may offer fee-free withdrawals with certain account types.

Tips for Using ATMs:

- **ATM Locations**: Use ATMs located at reputable banks, shopping centers, and hotels for added security.
- **Daily Limits**: Plan your withdrawals to stay within the daily withdrawal limits and avoid multiple fees.
- **Secure Transactions:** Cover the keypad when entering your PIN and be aware of your surroundings.

Using ATMs from reputable banks like Vietcombank and VietinBank provided secure and convenient access to cash. Checking with my home bank about international fees helped me plan my withdrawals and manage my budget effectively. Using ATMs in well-lit and secure locations added to my peace of mind during transactions.

Tipping Etiquette

Description: Tipping is not a traditional practice in Vietnam, but it is increasingly becoming common in the tourism and hospitality sectors. Understanding when and how to tip can help you show appreciation for good service.

Tipping Guidelines:

- **Restaurants**: Tipping is not obligatory, but leaving small change or rounding up the bill for good service is appreciated. In upscale restaurants, a tip of 5-10% of the bill is considered generous.
- **Hotels**: Tipping hotel staff, such as bellhops and housekeeping, is not required but appreciated. A small tip of 20,000-50,000 VND is a nice gesture for good service.
- **Tour Guides**: Tipping tour guides and drivers is common practice. Consider tipping around 50,000-100,000 VND per day for guides and 20,000-50,000 VND for drivers, depending on the quality of service.
- **Taxis**: Tipping taxi drivers is not expected, but rounding up the fare to the nearest 10,000 VND is a courteous gesture.

Tips for Tipping:

- **Discretion**: Offer tips discreetly and directly to the person you wish to thank.

- **Small Denominations**: Carry small denominations of VND for tipping, as larger bills may be difficult to change.
- **Personal Judgment**: Use your personal judgment and consider the quality of service when deciding whether to tip.

Leaving small tips at restaurants and rounding up taxi fares was appreciated and often met with gratitude from the service providers. Tipping tour guides and drivers for their excellent service added to the overall positive experience of the tours. Carrying small denominations of VND made it easy to offer tips discreetly and appropriately.

Communication and Connectivity

Staying connected while traveling in Vietnam is essential for navigating your trip, staying in touch with loved ones, and accessing important information. Understanding mobile networks and internet access, knowing useful apps for travelers, and ensuring you stay connected can greatly enhance your travel experience. In this section, we'll cover mobile networks and internet access, useful apps for travelers, and tips for staying connected.

Mobile Networks and Internet Access

Description: Vietnam has a well-developed telecommunications infrastructure, offering reliable mobile networks and widespread internet access. Here's what you need to know about staying connected in Vietnam:

Mobile Networks:
- **Major Providers**: The three main mobile network providers in Vietnam are Viettel, Mobifone, and Vinaphone. These providers offer extensive coverage and competitive rates for both calls and data.
- **SIM Cards**: Purchasing a local SIM card is an affordable and convenient way to stay connected. SIM cards can be bought at airports, mobile shops, and convenience stores. You'll need to present your passport for registration.
- **Data Plans**: Mobile data plans are available in various packages, ranging from daily to monthly plans. These plans offer generous data allowances at reasonable prices.

Internet Access:
- **Wi-Fi Availability**: Wi-Fi is widely available in hotels, cafes, restaurants, and public spaces. Many establishments offer free Wi-Fi for customers, making it easy to access the internet while on the go.
- **Internet Speed**: Internet speeds in urban areas are generally fast and reliable, while rural areas may have slower connections.
- **Internet Cafes**: Internet cafes are less common than they used to be, but they can still be found in some tourist areas and cities.

Tips for Mobile Networks and Internet Access:
- **Check Compatibility**: Ensure your mobile phone is unlocked and

compatible with Vietnamese networks before purchasing a local SIM card.
- **Choose a Reliable Provider**: Select a reputable mobile network provider with good coverage in the areas you'll be visiting.
- **Monitor Data Usage**: Keep track of your data usage to avoid running out of data unexpectedly. Many providers offer apps to help you monitor your usage.

Purchasing a local SIM card from Viettel at the airport provided excellent coverage and affordable data plans throughout my trip. Free Wi-Fi in cafes and hotels made it easy to stay connected and access important information. Monitoring my data usage with the provider's app helped me manage my data plan effectively.

Useful Apps for Travelers

Description: Using mobile apps can greatly enhance your travel experience in Vietnam by providing useful information, navigation, language translation, and more. Here are some essential apps for travelers:

Examples of Useful Apps:
1. **Grab**: A popular ride-sharing app that offers car and motorbike taxi services. It's a convenient and reliable way to get around cities and towns.
2. **Google Maps**: A navigation app that provides accurate maps, directions, and real-time traffic updates. It helps you find your way around and discover nearby attractions.
3. **Google Translate**: A language translation app that supports Vietnamese and can help you communicate with locals, translate signs, and understand menus.
4. **Trip Advisor**: An app that offers reviews, recommendations, and travel guides for hotels, restaurants, attractions, and tours. It helps you make informed decisions and plan your itinerary.
5. **Booking.com**: An app for booking accommodation, offering a wide range of options from hotels to guesthouses. It provides reviews, price comparisons, and easy booking features.
6. **XE Currency**: A currency conversion app that provides real-time exchange rates and helps you manage your budget by converting prices to your home currency.

Highlights:
- **Convenience:** Mobile apps provide convenient access to essential travel information and services.
- **Navigation and Directions:** Navigation apps help you find your way and explore new places with confidence.
- **Communication**: Translation apps assist with language barriers, making interactions with locals smoother and more enjoyable.

Using Grab for transportation provided reliable and affordable rides in cities like Hanoi and Ho Chi Minh City. Google Maps helped me navigate unfamiliar streets and find attractions, while Google Translate assisted with language barriers when ordering food and asking for directions. TripAdvisor and Booking.com were invaluable for planning my itinerary and booking accommodation. XE

Currency made it easy to manage my budget and convert prices on the go.

Staying Connected

Description: Staying connected with friends, family, and fellow travelers is important for both safety and enjoyment during your trip. Here are some tips for staying connected while traveling in Vietnam:

Communication Tips:
- **International Roaming**: Check with your home mobile provider about international roaming options and rates before traveling. Some providers offer affordable roaming packages.
- **Local SIM Card:** Purchasing a local SIM card is a cost-effective way to stay connected with local calls and data.
- **Messaging Apps:** Use messaging apps like WhatsApp, Viber, and Facebook Messenger to stay in touch with friends and family. These apps work well with Wi-Fi or mobile data.

Emergency Contacts:
- **Save Important Numbers:** Save the contact information of your accommodation, local emergency services, and your country's embassy or consulate in your phone.
- **Travel Insurance**: Keep your travel insurance details and emergency contact numbers handy in case of any emergencies.

Social Media and Sharing:
- **Share Your Location**: Share your travel itinerary and location with a trusted friend or family member for added security.
- **Post Updates**: Use social media to share updates and photos of your travels, keeping friends and family informed and connected.

Highlights:
- **Safety and Security:** Staying connected helps ensure your safety and allows you to seek assistance if needed.
- **Enjoyment**: Sharing your travel experiences with loved ones enhances the enjoyment of your trip.
- **Peace of Mind:** Keeping important contacts and emergency information accessible provides peace of mind.

Purchasing a local SIM card allowed me to stay connected with local calls and data at an affordable rate. Using messaging apps like WhatsApp and Facebook Messenger made it easy to communicate with friends and family. Sharing my travel itinerary and location with a trusted friend added an extra layer of security. Posting updates and photos on social media allowed me to share my experiences and stay connected with loved ones.

Sustainable Travel Tips

Traveling sustainably in Vietnam allows you to minimize your environmental impact and contribute positively to local communities. By adopting eco-friendly practices and supporting local initiatives, you can make a meaningful difference while enjoying your trip. In this section, we'll cover eco-friendly practices and ways to support local communities.

Eco-Friendly Practices

Description: Adopting eco-friendly practices during your travels helps protect the environment and preserve natural resources. Here are some tips for traveling sustainably in Vietnam:

1. **Reduce Plastic Use:**
   - Bring a reusable water bottle to refill instead of buying single-use plastic bottles. Many hotels and cafes offer refill stations.
   - Avoid using plastic bags and bring your own reusable shopping bag for purchases.
   - Say no to plastic straws and use a reusable straw if needed.
2. **Choose Eco-Friendly Accommodations:**
   - Look for hotels, guesthouses, and hostels that have eco-friendly practices, such as energy-efficient lighting, waste reduction programs, and water conservation measures.
   - Consider staying in eco-lodges or accommodations that support sustainability and conservation efforts.
3. **Use Sustainable Transportation:**
   - Opt for public transportation, such as buses and trains, to reduce your carbon footprint.
   - Rent bicycles or walk whenever possible to explore cities and towns in an eco-friendly way.
   - Use ride-sharing apps like Grab to share rides with others and reduce emissions.
4. **Minimize Energy and Water Consumption**:
   - Turn off lights, air conditioning, and electronic devices when not in use.
   - Take shorter showers and avoid unnecessary water usage.
   - Reuse towels and linens in hotels to reduce laundry-related water and energy consumption.
5. **Support Wildlife Conservation**:
   - Avoid activities that exploit or harm animals, such as elephant rides or visiting animal shows.
   - Choose responsible wildlife tours and sanctuaries that prioritize animal welfare and conservation.

Highlights:
- **Environmental Impact:** Eco-friendly practices help reduce your environmental impact and protect natural resources.
- **Sustainability**: Supporting eco-friendly accommodations and transportation options promotes sustainability in the travel industry.
- **Conservation**: Responsible travel choices contribute to the conservation of wildlife and natural habitats.

Bringing a reusable water bottle and shopping bag significantly reduced my plastic waste during my travels. Choosing eco-friendly accommodations in Hanoi and Hoi An provided comfortable stays while supporting sustainability efforts. Renting bicycles in Da Nang allowed me to explore the city in an eco-friendly and enjoyable way. Supporting responsible wildlife tours in Phong Nha-Ke Bang National Park contributed to the conservation of local wildlife.

Supporting Local Communities

Description: Supporting local communities during your travels ensures that your contributions have a positive and lasting impact on the people and culture of Vietnam. Here are some ways to support local communities:

1. **Shop Locally**:
   - Purchase souvenirs, handicrafts, and products from local markets and artisan shops. This supports local craftsmen and small businesses.
   - Avoid buying mass-produced items and focus on unique, handmade products that reflect the local culture.
2. **Eat Locally:**
   - Dine at local restaurants, food stalls, and family-run eateries. This supports local businesses and allows you to experience authentic Vietnamese cuisine.
   - Attend cooking classes to learn how to prepare traditional dishes using local ingredients.
3. **Choose Ethical Tours:**
   - Book tours and activities with local guides and operators who prioritize ethical practices and community involvement.
   - Look for tour companies that give back to the community and support social and environmental initiatives.
4. **Volunteer**:
   - Consider volunteering with local organizations or projects that benefit the community. This can include teaching English, participating in conservation efforts, or supporting community development projects.
   - Research volunteer opportunities in advance and choose reputable organizations.
5. **Respect Local Customs and Traditions:**
   - Show respect for local customs, traditions, and cultural practices. Dress modestly, especially when visiting religious sites, and be mindful of cultural norms.
   - Learn a few basic phrases in Vietnamese to show appreciation for the local language and culture.

Highlights:
- **Community Support:** Supporting local businesses and initiatives benefits the local economy and community development.
- **Cultural Experience**: Engaging with local communities provides a deeper understanding and appreciation of Vietnamese culture and traditions.
- **Ethical Travel**: Choosing ethical tours and volunteer opportunities promotes responsible and sustainable travel practices.

Shopping for souvenirs at local markets in Hanoi and Hoi An allowed me to support local artisans and bring home unique, handmade items. Dining at family-run eateries provided delicious and authentic Vietnamese cuisine while supporting local businesses. Participating in a cooking class in Ho Chi Minh City was a fun and educational experience that connected me with local food culture. Booking tours with ethical operators in the Mekong Delta ensured that my contributions had a positive impact on the community. Volunteering with a local organization in Sapa provided a meaningful way to give back and support community development projects.

Appendix

Useful Apps

Using mobile apps can greatly enhance your travel experience in Vietnam by providing useful information, navigation, language translation, and more. Here are some essential apps for travelers:

1. **Grab**: A popular ride-sharing app that offers car and motorbike taxi services. It's a convenient and reliable way to get around cities and towns.

2. **Google Maps:** A navigation app that provides accurate maps, directions, and real-time traffic updates. It helps you find your way around and discover nearby attractions.

3. **Google Translate:** A language translation app that supports Vietnamese and can help you communicate with locals, translate signs, and understand menus.

4. **Trip Advisor**: An app that offers reviews, recommendations, and travel guides for hotels, restaurants, attractions, and tours. It helps you make informed decisions and plan your itinerary.

5. **Booking.com**: An app for booking accommodation, offering a wide range of options from hotels to guesthouses. It provides reviews, price comparisons, and easy booking features.

6. **XE Currency**: A currency conversion app that provides real-time exchange rates and helps you manage your budget by converting prices to your home currency.

7. **Moovit**: A public transit app that provides information on bus routes, schedules, and transit directions in cities across Vietnam.

8. **Maps.me**: An offline map app that allows you to download maps and use them without an internet connection, making it useful for navigating remote areas.

9. **Skype**: A communication app that allows you to make voice and video calls, send messages, and share files with friends and family back home.

10. **Viber**: A messaging app that offers free text, voice, and video calls, making it easy to stay connected with loved ones.

Conclusion

Final Thoughts

As I look back on my journey through Vietnam, I am filled with a sense of nostalgia and gratitude for the incredible experiences I had in this beautiful and diverse country. Vietnam's rich cultural heritage, stunning landscapes, and warm hospitality left an indelible mark on my heart, and I cherish the memories of my travels there.

One of the highlights of my trip was the opportunity to explore Vietnam's vibrant cities. Hanoi, with its bustling Old Quarter, offered a sensory delight at every corner. The narrow streets were filled with the aroma of street food, the sound of motorbikes, and the sight of colorful markets. Enjoying a bowl of pho at a local eatery was a true culinary experience. The fragrant broth, tender beef, and fresh herbs combined to create a comforting and delicious meal that I will never forget. Wandering around Hoan Kiem Lake and visiting the historic Ngoc Son Temple provided a serene contrast to the city's lively atmosphere.

In Ho Chi Minh City, the energy and dynamism of the city were palpable. Exploring the bustling Ben Thanh Market was a treat for the senses, with its vibrant stalls offering everything from textiles to handicrafts to street food. The city's rich history came alive as I visited the War Remnants Museum and the Reunification Palace. The lively nightlife and modern skyscrapers showcased the city's contemporary spirit, while traditional dishes like banh mi and com tam offered a taste of its culinary heritage.

Vietnam's natural landscapes were nothing short of breathtaking. The emerald waters and limestone karsts of Ha Long Bay created a magical backdrop for kayaking and exploring hidden caves. The terraced rice fields of Sapa, with their vibrant green hues, provided a stunning setting for trekking and connecting with local ethnic minority communities. The warm hospitality of the villagers and the opportunity to learn about their traditions and way of life added depth to the experience.

The central region of Vietnam also held its own unique charm. Hoi An, with its lantern-lit streets and well-preserved architecture, felt like stepping back in time. The Hoi An Lantern Festival, where the town is illuminated with colorful lanterns, was a truly enchanting experience. Participating in a cooking class and learning to make traditional dishes like cao lau and banh xeo was a highlight, allowing me to bring a piece of Vietnamese cuisine back home.

Hue, the former imperial capital, offered a glimpse into Vietnam's royal past. Exploring the Imperial City and the royal tombs provided insights into the grandeur and history of the Nguyen

Dynasty. The city's signature dish, bun bo Hue, a spicy and flavorful noodle soup, was a culinary delight that I savored with every bite.

Throughout my travels, the kindness and warmth of the Vietnamese people stood out the most. Whether it was the friendly vendor at the market, the knowledgeable tour guide, or the hospitable family hosting me in their homestay, the genuine hospitality and smiles made me feel welcomed and appreciated. The cultural exchanges and conversations with locals enriched my journey and left me with a deep appreciation for Vietnam's people and traditions.

Traveling sustainably and supporting local communities added meaning to my journey. Shopping at local markets, dining at family-run eateries, and participating in ethical tours ensured that my contributions had a positive impact on the places I visited. It was heartening to see the efforts being made to preserve Vietnam's natural beauty and cultural heritage.

As I reminisce about my time in Vietnam, I am grateful for the unforgettable experiences, the breathtaking landscapes, the rich cultural heritage, and the warm connections I made. This incredible country, with its diverse offerings and welcoming spirit, will always hold a special place in my heart.

Thank you for joining me on this journey through Vietnam. May your travels be filled with wonder, discovery, and joy. Safe travels and enjoy every moment of your adventure in this extraordinary country!

Printed in Dunstable, United Kingdom